W9-ANO-111

Teacher Resource

Fast Ideas for Busy Teachers

Grades K–1

Published by Frank Schaffer Publications
an imprint of

 Children's Publishing

Editors: Donna Borst, Jeanine Manfro, Todd Sharp

Published by Frank Schaffer Publications
An imprint of McGraw-Hill Children's Publishing
Copyright © 2003 McGraw-Hill Children's Publishing

All Rights Reserved • Printed in the United States of America

Limited Reproduction Permission: Permission to duplicate these materials is limited to the person for whom they are purchased. Reproduction for an entire school or school district is unlawful and strictly prohibited.

Send all inquiries to:
McGraw-Hill Children's Publishing
3195 Wilson Drive NW
Grand Rapids, Michigan 49544

Fast Ideas for Busy Teachers—grades K–1
ISBN: 0-7682-2526-4

2 3 4 5 6 7 8 9 PHXBK 08 07 06 05 04 03

Table of Contents

Introduction for
Fast Ideas for Busy Teachers (K–1)

We know you've heard it a million times before, but *Fast Ideas for Busy Teachers* is really and truly the one resource that you just can't do without. We know what your life is like—running here and there all day long. By the end of the day you wonder if you actually got anything accomplished. We know you don't have time to go through 30 teacher resources looking for one little art project for Easter. We understand that when you're ready to start a study of community helpers, you don't want to search through file after file looking for that one new, fresh idea. You're just too busy—you know it and we know it. That's why this book is so perfect—everything you need is right at your fingertips.

We tried hard to think of everything. That's why you'll find ideas for every area of your curriculum, including language arts, math, science, social studies, and art. We also have some terrific activities that will help you get to know your students better. And if you're tired of the same old classroom decorations, you're going to love our section on classroom environment. It has everything from bulletin board ideas to room arrangements that will give you more space. Our intention is to take the frazzle out of your life, so take a deep breath, relax, and enjoy!

Getting Organized

Bucket Stools

Five-gallon plastic paint buckets make terrific stools for the classroom. Simply pad the lid and cover it with fabric. Elastic or glue around the edge will hold it in place. Store manipulatives such as blocks, milk lids, and small books inside. Paint supply stores often save buckets for schools if asked, or check restaurants where they often get food items in plastic buckets.

Order in the Classroom

Students can help you organize all their written assignments with this great idea. Purchase colorful file folders and print each student's name on one. Arrange the folders in alphabetical order in a brightly colored file crate. When students complete their written work, daily work, homework, or late assignments, they can file them in their folders for you to correct and record as your schedule allows. Young children will quickly learn about alphabetical order and assignments won't get lost.

Class Pictures

At the beginning of the school year, photocopy your students' individual photographs. Write each student's name under his picture for a pictorial attendance chart. This will come in handy for you and for substitutes throughout the year.

Student Mailboxes

Shoe organizers work great as student mailboxes in the classroom. Label each opening with a student's name and it becomes her very own mailbox. As papers are graded, file them in the mailboxes and at the end of each day, students know right where to go to pick up their papers.

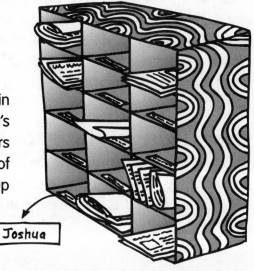

Joshua

Getting Organized

Name Chart

At the front of your classroom, post an alphabetical list of the students in your class. When students do their daily journal writing, they can refer to the list to see how to spell their friends' names. They love to write about one another and now they won't have to ask for your help in doing so.

Grade Book at a Glance

Write passing grades in your grade book in red and failing grades in black ink. This helps prepare for quick conferences and report cards. You can also put tabs on the pages of the grade book to make it easy to prepare report cards and to find various subjects. This simple practice can save a lot of time.

Bag 'em!

Keep children from playing with pencils, crayons, erasers, and other items by using zip-close plastic bags. Tape a bag to the side of each child's desk, and place items from desks that might be played with in the bags.

Keeping Track of Puzzles

Help students clean up puzzles easily by coding the pieces of each puzzle. Use colors, numbers, or symbols. For example, mark a puzzle box with a star on the lid. Then mark the back of each puzzle piece with the same star. Later, if you or a student finds a stray puzzle piece, simply look on the back for the code and match it to the correct puzzle box. Puzzle cleanup will be faster, and there won't be any more missing pieces.

Organizing with Stickers

Organize posters and hang-ups by putting a color-coded circle sticker on the back of each. This way you will know which box you got the item from by matching the sticker to the box. Keep an index card (also marked) with a list of the items in each box. This will make filing much easier.

Cooperative Learning Groups

If your class does most of its work in cooperative learning groups, seating arrangements can be a challenge. To help with this, put every child's name on a card using four different ability levels and four different colors of cards. Try to get a child from each group or color at a table. It's also good to identify those children who need more socialization and team them up accordingly. On the cards, include the group or table numbers where the students have previously sat so everyone gets a new group and seat when it's time to switch. With four or five children in a group, you should get a nice mix. It's also easy to shuffle the cards when you're ready for new groups.

Stash Packs

Use tummy tote bags to improve classroom management. Ask students and parents to donate used pouches or look for inexpensive ones at yard sales. Fill one with pencils, or pens, and markers to strap on a chair at the art or writing center. Fill another bag with extra staples, thumbtacks, scissors, and so on to wear when you're working on a bulletin board outside your room. In another bag, stash first aid and sewing materials to take on field trips. Prepare and use other stash packs as your needs dictate.

Mark each bag with a laminated label and keep them in a crate or on a shelf with the labels visible. Nearby, post a list of the bags' contents. This will help student helpers determine which supplies need to be restocked when the packs are used.

Paper Plate Mailboxes

Cut a paper plate in half and then staple one half to a full-sized paper plate to form a pocket. Let students each decorate one with their names, stickers, etc. Tape the mailboxes on the back of student desks. The mailboxes take up no extra space and cost only pennies.

Getting Organized

Color-Coded Name Tags

Color-code each child's name on his desk. The color of the name tells the child's reading group. A colored circle tells that child's math group.

Publishing Center Organizer

Organize supplies at your publishing center the easy way! Paste a piece of colorful construction paper in the bottom of a cardboard soft-drink tray. Trace and label the publishing materials as shown. When students use the stapler, for example, they can put it back in exactly the right spot.

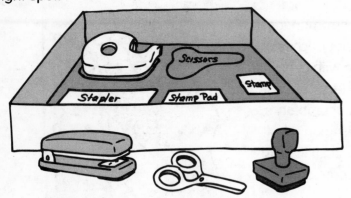

Desk Organizers

Gather cardboard trays (such as the trays that are in the bottom of cases of canned drinks) from the grocery store. Give each student a tray to use as a "desk drawer." Students can keep all their loose odds and ends in the tray and pull it out like a drawer whenever needed.

Cardboard Clipboards

Clipboards will come in handy all day long in your busy classroom. Students can use them whenever they need a firm writing surface away from their desks. Clip a clothespin to a 10" x 12" (25.4 cm x 30.5 cm) cardboard rectangle and attach a pencil. Make one for each student and store them in a box or basket.

Handy-Dandy Recycled Lunchboxes

Ask students to bring to school lunchboxes they no longer use. The lunchboxes make sturdy, colorful storage boxes for scissors, manipulatives, activity cards, and all sorts of other classroom materials and supplies.

Stand-Up Display for Students' Work

Tape 15 file folders together to create this handy stand-up display. Write each student's name on a clothespin and clip the clothespins on the display. Place the display on a countertop in your classroom. Let children hang up their work themselves. This is a great way to allow students to take responsibility for changing from time to time the work they have on display.

"Box-It" Storage System

Remove tops and about 2/3 of the cardboard from one side of various cereal or cracker boxes (see example). Fasten the boxes together with tape or brads and label each box with a student's name. The boxes are perfect storage bins for students' works-in-progress.

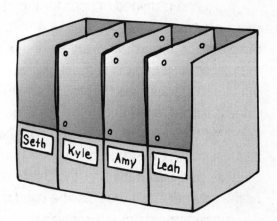

Recess-Duty Hip Packs

Keep a hip pack supplied with sunglasses, tissues, bandages, surgical gloves, and a marker, notepad, and whistle. When you have recess duty, snap the pack on and go.

Wallpaper Shapes

Obtain several wallpaper sample books and keep them in your classroom. The wallpaper can be used to make seasonal shapes (apples, hearts, etc.) to put on calendars. You can also use the shapes in a discussion about solid, floral, plaid, and striped designs.

Getting Organized

Yarn Storage

Here is another handy use for those five-gallon ice cream cartons. Store three or four different colors of yarn inside the container. Draw flowers on the outside of the carton. The color of each flower should correspond to the color of one ball of yarn inside the carton. Cut a hole for each color in the lid and thread the yarn through the hole. You will have a tangle-proof yarn dispenser that will last for years!

Clothespin Clips

You'll find a myriad of uses for this simple-to-make classroom organizer. Cut enough 3" x 4" (7.6 cm x 10.1 cm) pieces of colored tagboard for everyone in your class and laminate the pieces. Use contact cement to glue a spring-type clothespin to the back of each card. Write student names on self-adhesive labels and attach labels to the tagboard. Use these handy clothespin clips to display student artwork on a clothesline that is strung across the room. When work samples are hung from the line, the child's name is as prominent as the artwork. Clips may also be used to hold together unfinished assignments or to organize the teacher's desk. Hint: If the cards are laminated, the labels can be peeled off and the clips used over and over again!

Missing Scissors Solution

Almost every teacher wastes valuable classroom time searching for lost scissors. Try this simple solution: Ask each child to bring a long shoelace to class. Tie one end to the scissors and the other end to the student's desk. Children can still use their scissors easily and they fit neatly into desks when not in use. This simple tip will eliminate all scissor-related confusion in your classroom.

Pencil Number-Off

Keep track of pencils by assigning each child in your class a number. Using a permanent marker, write each child's number on her pencil near the eraser end. When a pencil is dropped or misplaced, it is put in a can labeled "Missing Pencils." Children check the container to locate lost pencils. If a lot of pencils end up in the can, you may want to call out the pencil numbers.

Marking Used Pages

After making copies of a reproducible work-book page for students, mark it with a small self-sticking note. This is an easy way to remember which workbook pages you have used. The notes are easy to remove and can be reused.

Quick Workbook Check

Try this simple idea for keeping workbooks up-to-date. When a student is absent and misses a workbook assignment, put a bright, solid-colored sticker on the front cover. On the sticker, write the page numbers the student needs to complete. This serves as a visual reminder both for you and for the student. After the pages are finished and checked, remove the sticker.

Folders for Absent Children

Eliminate confusion and help children who have been absent make up assignments by creating "Absent Folders." Decorate file folders with stickers and label them. When a child is absent, assign another child the task of placing an Absent Folder on the missing student's desk. Ask her to write down daily assignments from the board and place them in the folder. Worksheets may also be placed in the Absent Folder, which will be ready and waiting for the returning child.

Waiting Folders

Give each student in your class a folder that contains extra assignments to do when class work is finished early. The worksheets should be fun, but educational, and each child should be given work according to her academic ability. This prevents less capable students from becoming frustrated with work that is too difficult, and it keeps more capable students challenged. The left side of the folder contains the unfinished work. When they complete the work, students should put it in the right side of the folder. When you collect the folders on Friday, give each student a sticker for each completed paper and replace the completed papers with new ones for next week. Pages needing corrections are put back on the left side of the folder for students to correct.

Getting Organized

The Case of the Lost Pencil

To cure a chronic case of lost pencils, construct a simple pencil holder for your class. Turn an egg carton upside down and label each cup with a child's names. Poke a pencil through each cup. Make sure that each child places his pencil in the proper spot before leaving for home. A helper can have all the pencils sharpened and ready for the next day.

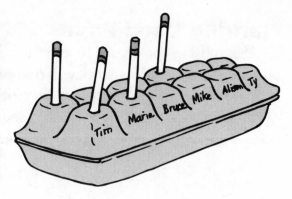

Be a Neatnik!

Avoid classroom clean-up blahs and turn dismissal into fun. Announce, "It's Neatnik Time!" Set a timer for five to ten minutes and watch students begin cleaning the room. After they finish, students sit in a quiet circle to show they are ready for inspection. When the timer sounds, the whole class must be "Neatnik-ready" for a class sticker award. Make a numbered chart. Each time a sticker is presented, place it over a number on the chart. After five numbers are covered, the class may receive a special privilege. This is a great way to teach group responsibility and have fun doing it.

Can It!

Spray-paint a gallon-sized vegetable can for each student. (Ask your school cafeteria manager to save these for your class.) Let each student choose the color her can will be painted. Let students decorate the cans using paint pens and other craft materials, and personalize them with their names. Let them keep the cans in the class to hold their supplies. Or have students design cans to take home to their moms, dads, or favorite people.

Binders for Portfolio Assessment

Binders are a great way to store student work. They are easy to manage and display for teacher and parent assessment. Binders allow the flexibility to group work together and shuffle papers back and forth. Use a three-hole punch to convert all necessary student work to binder format. Write the students' names on the spines of the binders and file them in library fashion. Use peel-off labels to keep monthly records of student progress. Keep labels easily accessible on your desk to note student behavior and work, and then transfer the notes to the inside of the binders at the end of each month. If you decide to use the same binders year after year, simply tape students' names to the spines so they can be changed at the beginning of each school year.

Environment

Tulip Garland

Have children cut tulip pictures from catalogs, glue them to construction paper, and then trim around the flowers. Help each child punch a hole on each side of the pictures. String the tulips together using paper clips or yarn for a spring garland. You can also use the patterns on the next page to make your garland. Cut the tulips from colored construction paper or give students patterns and let them color the flowers as they wish. Hang the garland around the door or in the windows to welcome spring.

How Many Is 100?

Prepare a bulletin board with the title "How Many Is 100?" Have students help fill the board with 100 objects arranged in 10 rows of 10 each. Copy paper shapes such as hearts, circles, triangles, and so on, on colored construction paper and have students cut them out to place on the board.

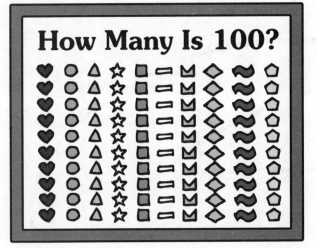

Action Tree

Don't throw that bulletin board Christmas tree away! Recycle it to use throughout the year. Let children help decorate the tree for a variety of themes. Have them bring pictures from home that begin with the sound of a particular letter you are studying. Challenge them to find pictures of mammals to hang on the tree to make it a "mammal" tree. For younger children, turn the tree into a color tree and encourage them to hang pictures and ornaments with only that color on it. For Valentine's Day, encourage children to draw pictures or bring photos of their families to hang on the tree for a "family" tree.

Let your students help decide what theme to give the tree each month. Keep everyone actively learning year-round.

Favorite Things Bulletin Board

Play a tape of the song "My Favorite Things" from *The Sound of Music*. Cut out letters for the bulletin board caption: "These Are Our Favorite Things!" Attach them to the middle of the board at the top. Hand out art paper, pencils, and crayons. Have children draw pictures of some of their favorite things such as friends, pets, foods, and activities. Ask each child to print a sentence about that item at the bottom of the picture. Mount the pictures on the board in an attractive arrangement. Cut some music notes from black paper and add them to the board.

Tulip Patterns

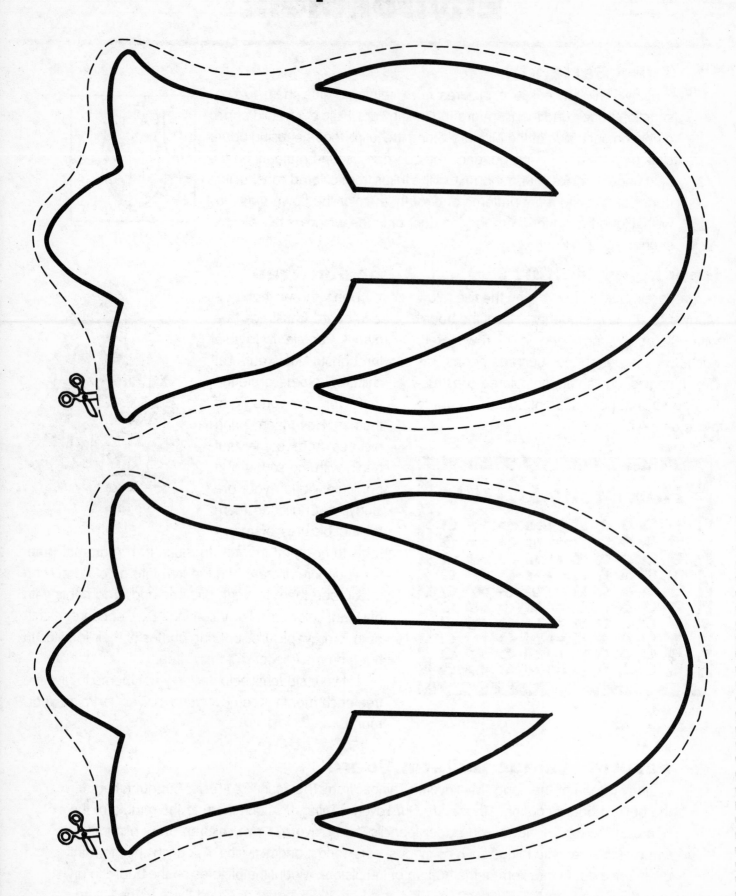

The A-B-Cs of Classroom Beauty

Are you looking for simple, low-cost ways to beautify your classroom? Try these ideas and you'll love the difference!

A stands for a place for everything and everything in its place. Purchase durable, cheap, plastic storage containers in a monochromatic color scheme. See how much more attractive your classroom becomes.

B stands for bring nature in, whether by adding beautiful green or flowering plants or pictures that represent the joy and beauty of nature. Encourage your students to bring in items of nature that they find.

C stands for color. Do you want a vibrant, energetic atmosphere in your classroom? Then use the primary reds, yellows, and blues—even the new neon shades that are available. If you prefer a calmer, more eye-pleasing approach, choose a color such as green or pale blue. Look for classroom accessories or use decorative, adhesive plastic in a variety of soft shades to unify your little corner of the world.

King of the Dads

A male emperor penguin is a great dad. He helps to incubate his unborn chick by holding the egg on his feet. He also helps feed and care for the young penguin when it hatches.

Take the opportunity to highlight students' dads or other special men in their lives for their special qualities. Give each student a sheet of writing paper on which to explain why his or her dad is the greatest. The student should describe (and illustrate) specific ways Dad helps him or her.

Display these tributes on a bulletin board. You may want to include some photos of these special men (both penguins and people).

Environment

A Class Reading Aquarium

Create a Reading Aquarium in your classroom. Cover a bulletin board with light blue paper for water. Add precut aquarium rocks, seaweed, etc., to make the aquarium look real. Caption the bulletin board, "Our Class Reading Aquarium." Randomly place six large, precut, laminated fish in six different colors on the background. Write one of the following captions on each fish: "Books Read by Teacher"; "Books Read by Principal"; "Books Read by Librarian"; "Books Read by Parents"; "Books Read by Staff"; and "Books Read by Visitors."

For each large fish, cut ten small fish in the same color. Every time a book is read to your students, record the title on a small fish in the color appropriate to the reader. For example, a book read by the teacher would be recorded on a small fish the same color as the large fish that says "Books Read by Teacher."

Attach each small fish on the bulletin board near the large fish of the same color. As more and more books are read, "schools" of fish will appear.

Somewhere on the bulletin board, add a large fish in a seventh color. On this fish, write the questions listed below. Use these questions with the class at the end of each week.

Which people or groups have read the same number of books as us?
Who has read the most books as us?
Who has read the fewest books?
How many different schools of fish do we have?
Name the color of each school of fish.
How many large fish in our aquarium? How many small fish?

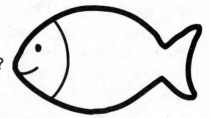

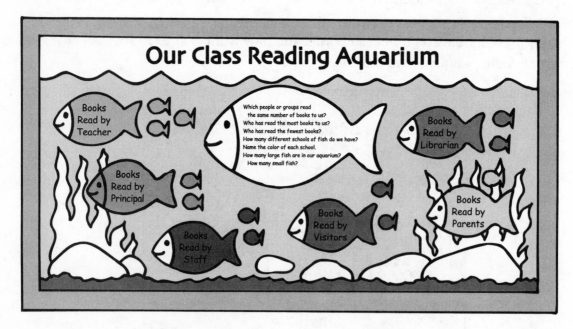

Our Class Reading Aquarium

Cool Door Décor

For a quick way to decorate your classroom door in the hot summer months, have the children make paper ice cream cones showing their favorite flavors. Have the children tape their cones randomly on the classroom door. Then post a title that says, "We're a Cool Class" and tape a class picture under it.

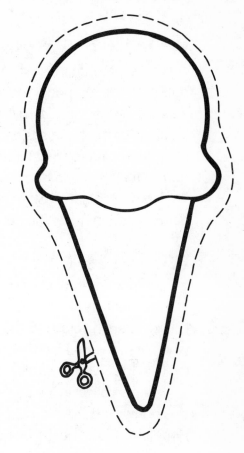

You Are What You Eat

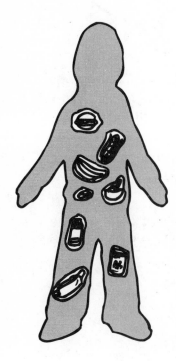

Trace each child's body outline on a large sheet of butcher paper. Have the students cut out the outlines. Provide time for the students to sort through magazines and cut out pictures of their favorite foods. Tell the students to arrange their pictures neatly on their paper bodies. When they are finished arranging, have the students glue their pictures inside the outline. Display these in the classroom or hallway.

Apple Tree

On the first day of school, take a photograph of each student. Mount photos on apples made of construction paper. Cut out a tree from construction paper and display the apples on the tree. Label the board "The Whole Bunch." Save the apples to send home in a memory book at the end of the year. This is an excellent bulletin board or display for the hall.

Environment

Welcome "Bright" New Students

Create a three-dimensional sun from yellow tissue paper. Use scrap paper to add details such as eyes, sunglasses, and so on. Cut rays from construction paper and make them three-dimensional by scoring the paper down the middle and folding. Write a child's name on each ray and attach around the sun. Title the bulletin board "Welcome Bright New Students." Children and parents will beam when they see the names shining out at them.

Whose Is This?

Label an area of your classroom "Whose Is This?" and place a box in the area (or simply put the label on the box). Draw an owl on the box. Explain to children that this is the "Lost and Found" area in your classroom. If someone finds something on the floor and doesn't know to whom it belongs, it may be put in this box. If someone needs to find a lost item, where do they look? In the "Whose Is This?" box!

If items collect in the box without being claimed, take a couple of minutes at the end of the class now and then to hold up each item and have children say with you, "Whose is this?" Hopefully, you'll find the owner.

I Can Grow

Start your school year with this eye-catching and positive display. Make a large tree trunk from brown paper. Paint small paper plates green for leaves, one for each student and one for yourself. Cut out an apple shape for each student and yourself (pattern can be found on page 17). Mount a photograph on an apple. Attach each apple with a paper clip to a paper plate. Next, discuss with students some of the things they can do—count to 100, recite the alphabet, give their phone numbers, and so on. Have each child tell you something he can do and write it on his leaf.

This is a wonderful display to help start the year on a positive note. Students will get the idea that they can do lots of things and will learn to do even more throughout the year.

At Home in the Ocean

Children may think ocean animals can live anywhere in the ocean. Help them understand that ocean animals are suited for living in different ocean habitats with this attractive display. Jellyfish float along the surface of the ocean, mammals and fish are well-adapted for swimming in the open sea, and animals like lobsters and snails live on the shallow ocean floor.

Have your children make stuffed ocean animals to create an ocean habitat bulletin board. Children color or paint an ocean animal on butcher paper. Then they cut it out and use it as a pattern to trace a back. After cutting out the back, children staple together the two pieces, leaving an opening. Stuff the animal with newspaper and then staple the opening.

Use different colors of butcher paper to create a bulletin board that shows the open sea, the shore and the ocean floor. Ask students to bring the animals to the bulletin board and tell where they should be placed. Then, attach the animals for a colorful display.

Fun with Shapes

During a unit on shapes, head a bulletin board with "What Shape Am I? Name Ten Places You Can Find Me." Draw large simple pictures of the basic shapes and make them into characters. Place one shape at a time on the bulletin board. Change the shape every few days. Students can write the solutions when they have free time.

The Children's Own Bulletin Board

Divide a large bulletin board into sections and label each section with a student's name. This bulletin board provides each student with a personal spot for displaying her work throughout the year. Leave a few spots blank in case you need them for new students.

Linear Calendar

Cut lengths of tagboard 6" (15.2 cm) high and staple them together to form one long strip. Write the days and months of the school year on the strips. Punch a hole near each date. Mount the calendar on a wall or under the chalkboard. Hang samples of student work, test reminders, field trip dates, student birthdays, etc. At the end of the school year, your students will have an interesting record of their work and activities. You can leave the calendar up for next year by simply removing the previous year's material when the new school year begins.

Environment

Color Train

This is a color-filled bulletin board idea. Cut out eight "cars" from colored construction paper and label each car appropriately: red, orange, green, blue, yellow, purple, brown, and black. Cut out and label items that are associated with a particular color from construction paper (purple grapes, green tree, red apple). Attach these objects to three cars marked "seek and find." Students have fun matching color words by selecting items from the "seek and find" cars and placing them in the correct cars on the train.

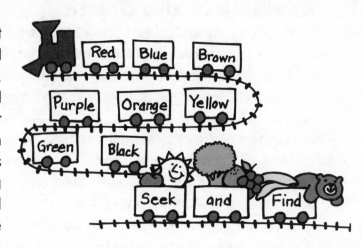

Krazy Kites

What could be more fun during the windy months than a colorful bulletin board filled with kites? Have students cut out diamond shapes from different colors of construction paper. Decorate the kites with crayons or felt tip pens. Or, students can draw pictures of their faces and mount them on the kites. For older children, have them write a short story about the wind on lined writing paper. Stories are then mounted on the kites. Add colored yarn for kite tails and tissue paper for ties. Cover the bulletin board with sky-blue construction paper and add a few white clouds. Hang the kites.

Famous Folks

February is the ideal time for remembering the men and women who helped make America great. However, this bulletin board can be used anytime you want to teach your students about some of our heroes in history. Each student selects a famous American to honor on a commemorative postage stamp. They may skim through reference books to select their subjects or you may post a list of people and have students choose. After students draw portraits of their famous Americans, paste the pictures on colored construction paper and cut the edges to look like stamp perforations. You might ask each student to give a brief oral report about his famous person.

Friends Bulletin Board

Here's a unique way to recognize a different student each week and build self-esteem. Ask students to bring photos of themselves, or use an instant camera to take a photo of each student. Each week, display a different child's photo at the center of a bulletin board with the child's name above the photo and the phrase "is in my circle of friends because …" below the photo. Give every student in the class a "friend" pattern. Students should write on their patterns positive characteristics that they enjoy or admire about the "student of the week." Mount the "friends" comments in a circle around the featured student.

Our Handiwork Bulletin Board

In three corners of the board, place small posters that say:
"Lend a (picture of hand),"
"Give a (picture of hand)," and
"Hold a (picture of hand)."
Trace, label, and cut out each child's hand and print her name on it. Then have each child draw a self-portrait on a piece of paper and color the frame. Attach the children's hands next to their handiwork. If possible, add a border with hands on it. Discuss the importance of helping by lending a hand, giving a hand, and sometimes, holding a hand.

Environment

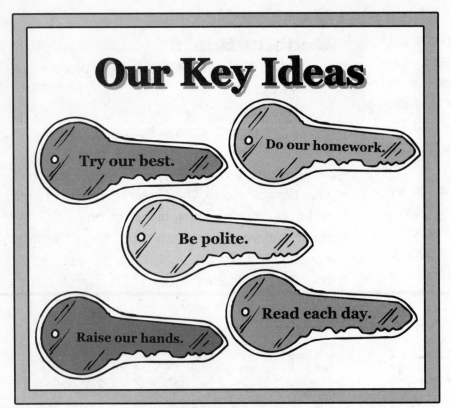

Our Key Ideas Bulletin Board

At the beginning of a new school year, display the bulletin board title and blank laminated keys. Let children work together to come up with rules or ideas they would like to achieve in the coming year. Write their ideas on the laminated keys with wipe-off markers so you can change and adapt your goals as the year progresses.

As you use this board year after year, notice which of the ideas and rules change and which remain the same.

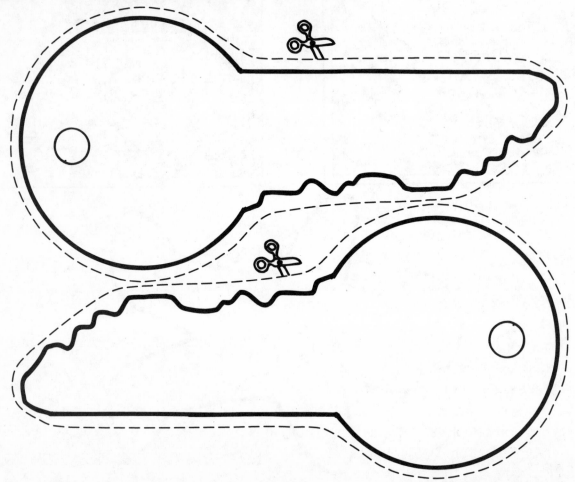

Garden of Learning

Show off your students' accomplishments. Have each child place his closed hand in a dish of tempera paint. Have each child stamp the closed handprint on construction paper that is about the same color as the paint to make a tulip bud print. Outline the print in black and add a few petal lines. Have each student cut out the bud and cut a green paper stem. Demonstrate how to trace around your three middle fingers to make a leaf shape. Direct each child to cut out several leaves and to write something special that she learned on each leaf. Have each child glue the parts of the tulip together. Dress up your tulip garden bulletin board with a white picket fence.

Scarecrow Says . . .

This is a great fall bulletin board that can be used to decorate your room as well as find out what your students did over the summer.

Reproduce the patterns on page 24 so that each child has a set. Have children color the scarecrow's hat, shirt, pants, and pumpkin head using fall colors. Then have them cut out the pieces and glue them together to make their scarecrow. Have students write a sentence about something they did over the summer vacation on the caption piece.

Animals Come in All Shapes

Geometric animals make an eye-catching display. Provide construction-paper shapes (circles, ovals, squares, triangles, rectangles, and diamonds) in lots of sizes and colors. Have each child put some shapes together to make an animal. Let the students arrange the shapes on contrasting construction paper and glue them down. They can cut around the animal shapes if they want. Show off the completed menagerie on a bulletin board titled "Animals Come in All Shapes."

Scarecrow Patterns

© McGraw-Hill Children's Publishing

0-7682-2526-4 *Fast Ideas for Busy Teachers*

Our Class Yearbook

End the school year with a bulletin board full of memories. Start by thinking back over the year together and listing the events and activities that stick out in your students' minds. Direct the children each to choose something that the class did during the year and draw a "photo" of it on a copy of the pattern provided page 26. Have the students write captions for their photos. Younger children can dictate their captions. Post the photos on a large open book shape under the title "Our Class Yearbook." If there's room, add to the yearbook real photographs that you've taken of your students or of class activities. Everyone will enjoy standing around this board reminiscing.

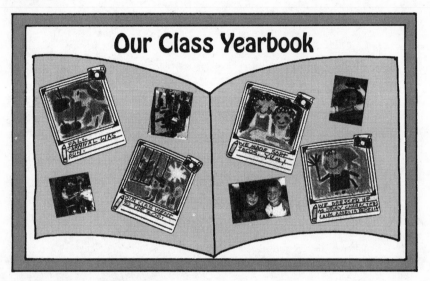

Papers to Crow About

Use this bulletin board to show off your students' work. Reproduce the patterns found on page 27 on tagboard. Give each student a set of the patterns. Students should first cut out the patterns (if possible) and then trace the patterns on black paper. They should then cut out the crow and beak. Next, have them draw eyes on the crow with white crayon and fold and attach the beak. Place the crows along a piece of string stretched across the bulletin board. Finally, hang excellent papers under the crow's feet.

Our Class Yearbook Pattern

© McGraw-Hill Children's Publishing

0-7682-2526-4 *Fast Ideas for Busy Teachers*

Papers to Crow About Patterns

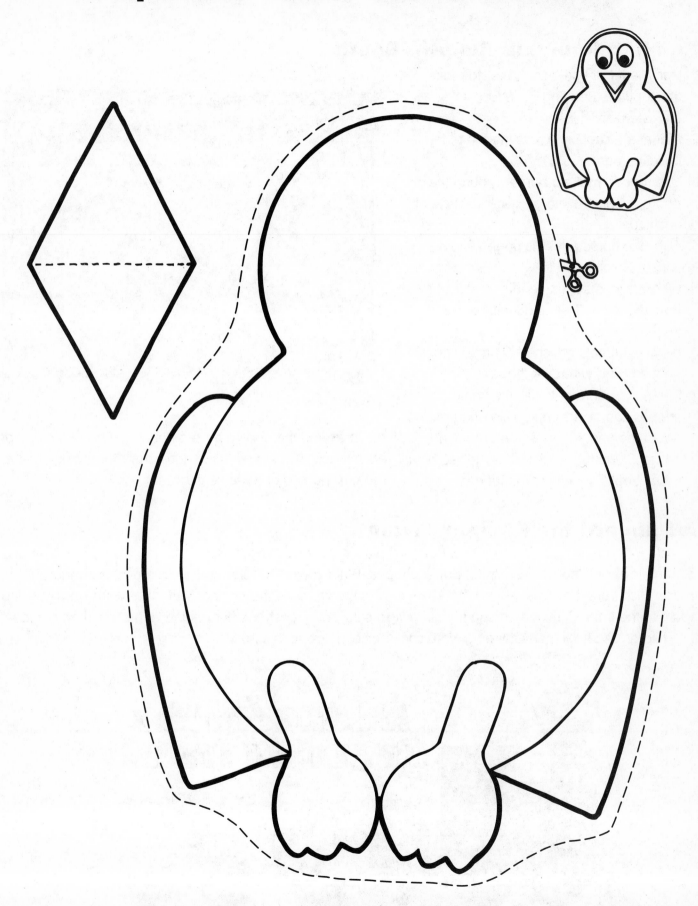

Environment

Reading Roundup Bulletin Board

1. Hand letter or use a computer to make the caption, "Reading Roundup," in a western style.
2. Mount the caption across the top of the bulletin board.
3. Use rope to make a border around the board, looping it into a lasso-like circle at each corner.
4. Copy the horse patterns page 29 in a variety of colors.
5. When students finish reading books, have them write the titles and their names on the horse shapes.
6. Let the students attach their horse shapes on the board wherever they like.
7. When the board gets full, the horse shapes can be saved in a file and handed out at the end of the year to be taken home. Students will be excited to see how many books they have rounded up.

To extend the activity, have a Roundup Day at the end of each week. Ask students to share orally the books they've read, using two or three sentences.

All Aboard the Rhyming Train

Add to this bulletin board as your students discover more rhyming words. First, make a train engine and a number of cars from construction paper shapes. Write a word on the engine and post it on the bulletin board. Elicit from the class a word that rhymes with the word on the engine. Write that word on a car and add it to the train. Continue adding rhyming word cars. Later, post another engine with a word on it and let the children see how many rhyming word cars they can add to this train.

Reading Roundup Patterns

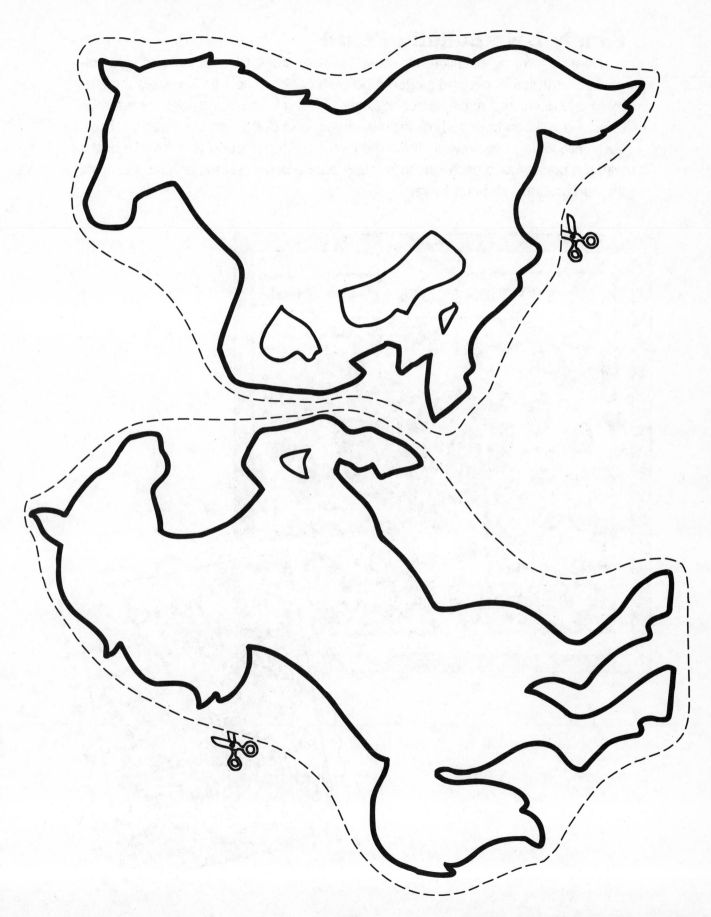

© McGraw-Hill Children's Publishing

29

0-7682-2526-4 *Fast Ideas for Busy Teachers*

Environment

Family Love Bulletin Board

Here's a fun way for children to make family portraits. Give the children light-colored construction paper and gingerbread men cookie cutters (in two sizes if possible). Have each child make one cookie cutter tracing for each member of his family. Direct the children to draw hair, facial features, and clothes on each person. Have each child write, "I love my family." at the top of the paper. Cover your bulletin board with red paper. Hang each student's family on the board. Let the children decorate the background with heart stickers.

Getting to Know Your Students

Web of Friendship

Start the school year by spinning a web of friendship. During the first week, have a discussion with students about friends and friendship. Then give each student a sheet of paper that has a large spider web drawn on it. The web should have enough "spaces" in the design so each child in the class can sign her name. Direct students to move around the classroom, asking each classmate to be a friend and to sign his name in one of the web's spaces. At the end of the activity, every student should have a web filled with signatures of friendship—including the teacher's.

Jump-Starting a New Year

The beginning of a new school year can be an exciting but apprehensive time for many students. To help welcome the new students into your class, send a letter to each child the week prior to the start of school. In the letter, tell the child that you are eager to meet him or her and are interested to know what the child did over the summer. Encourage children to bring a photo, drawing, or souvenirs of their summer vacations. Then, when the big day arrives, each new student has a "summer show-and-tell" ready to go. This makes introductions easier too.

Getting to Know You

Begin your new school year by having students print their first names in black marker vertically down the left side of sheets of penmanship paper. Their homework is to take the name sheet home and create an acrostic of words that describe them. Each word they use must begin with one of the letters of their name. When the homework is brought back the next day, collect the papers and put them in a box. Choose one to read aloud, but don't reveal the student's name. The class may guess who the student is from the descriptive words. Whoever guesses the student's name gets to choose another paper and read the descriptive words (without reading the name) to the class.

Getting to Know Your Students

Class Act

Take a photograph of each student in your classroom using a digital camera. Give each student a sheet of paper with everyone's photo on it. Have students cut apart the photos and arrange them in a variety of ways.

- In alphabetical order by first name
- In alphabetical order by last name
- By birthday
- By hair color
- By eye color
- By favorite activity

Baby Pictures

Make a bulletin board displaying students' baby pictures. Don't identify them by name—only by number. Try and guess which student belongs to each photograph.

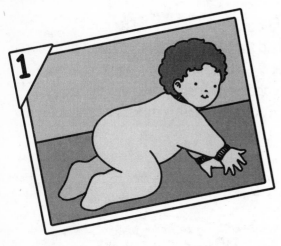

No Bones About It

At the beginning of the year, give each student in your class a dog bone shape made out of white construction paper. Ask them to write their names and five words that they think describe themselves. Mount the bones on the bulletin board and read them together so that you can all learn about one another. Title the board "No Bones About It—We're Going to Have a Great Year!"

Photo Family Tree

Start off your school year with a fun family project. Send a photo frame cut from construction paper to each family. Ask them to fill it with pictures of the family, friends, grandparents, pets, and so on.

When the frames are returned to school, have students tell about themselves. At the same time, you will gain knowledge about your new students.

Have students write a few sentences about their photos. Attach writing papers to the frames and hang them in the hall for everyone to see.

Getting to Know Your Students

Book of Records

At the beginning of the year, help students get acquainted with one another by compiling a classroom Book of Records. Survey students to find out who has traveled the furthest, who has attended the most schools, who has the most siblings, and so on until every student holds a record. Then have each student draw a picture and write a sentence describing her record-breaking feat. Assemble the pages into a book and keep it in the classroom library.

Summertime Clocks

This simple project is a good sharing activity for the first week of school. Give each child a paper plate, paper scraps, and a brass fastener. Then have the children follow these directions:

1. Write "Summertime" and your name on the back of the paper plate.
2. Make two clock hands from paper.
3. Attach the hands to the front of the clock with the brass fastener.
4. Use a crayon and divide the front of the clock into three equal sections.
5. Label each section with one of these topics— "Things I Did," "People I Met," and "Places I Went."

Have children respond to each topic by writing a sentence or drawing a picture in each section. Finally, have students take turns sharing the information on their clocks.

Beach Ball Name Game

Have the students stand in a circle. Pass a beach ball around as you sing these words to the tune of "Bingo."

> There is a classmate kind and good,
> And _____ is his/her name-o.
> _____ is a good friend,
> _____ is a good friend,
> _____ is a good friend,
> And _____ is his/her name-o.

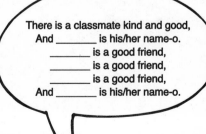

There is a classmate kind and good,
And _____ is his/her name-o.
_____ is a good friend,
_____ is a good friend,
_____ is a good friend,
And _____ is his/her name-o.

Fill in the blanks with a student's name. The student holding the ball at the end of the song gets her name put in the song next. Sing until everyone's name is used.

Getting to Know Your Students

What's My Game?

In this game, the class sings new words to the tune of "The Farmer in the Dell." Each new verse says a student's name and what activity he enjoys. As the class sings the verse, the child whom the class sings about must say the name of the "game" she likes best and pantomime the activity. Begin the game by first singing about yourself to the class. Then the whole class sings a verse about each child. For example, lead the children in singing the following:

> Mrs. Forest is my name,
> Mrs. Forest is my name,
> Hey, ho, oh, do you know
> That tennis is my game?

While singing the last verse, pretend you are a tennis player hitting a ball. Then choose a student to sing about and have the class join in the singing as follows:

> Miss Katie is her name,
> Miss Katie is her name,
> Hey, ho, oh, do you know
> That . . .

Have "Katie" fill in the name of her favorite activity and pantomime it. The song then moves on to another student and continues this way until all the students have had a chance to act out an activity.

> Mrs. Forest is my name,
> Mrs. Forest is my name,
> Hey, ho, oh, do you know
> That tennis is my game?

Behavior Management

You Deserve a Hand!

How often do you say to your students, *You deserve a hand*? To encourage deserving students, give each a construction paper hand that you tape to the child's shirt to wear all day. The hand says, "I deserve a hand for my efforts today."

Students are proud and enthusiastic about wearing the hands and are given opportunities to tell about their hard work or good deeds when children from other classes see the hands and ask, "What did you do to deserve a hand?"

Hands may be given for a variety of reasons: hard work, attentiveness, good manners, sharing, helping someone, and so on. Make sure you keep a large supply of hands "on hand" since students will want to wear them home for parents to see.

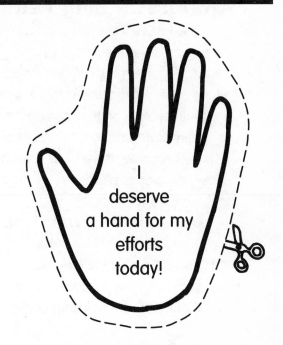

I deserve a hand for my efforts today!

Ways to Be a Good Friend

When your students are not kind to one another, talk about friendship and how to be a good friend. Here are some good ideas to get you started:

- Read the book *Stone Soup* by Marcia Brown (Scott Foresman, 1989) and then write Souper Friendship Recipes. You can even make soup in class together. Try graphing the ways friends solve their problems.
- Make puppets and act out in cooperative groups some of the problems that friends may have and what they can do to solve these problems.
- Each week, assign each student a new buddy. Buddies are encouraged to do nice things for one another. During class discussions, buddies share what they do with one another.
- Teach the children the following song that is sung to the tune of "Pop Goes the Weasel."

Don't walk around with your nose in the air,
Don't think you're better than others.
A time may come when things go wrong,
You'll need your brothers.

Don't walk around with your nose in the air.
Treat others, as you should do,
Or you may end up by yourself
With no one beside you.

Behavior Management

Understanding Feelings

To effectively resolve conflicts, your students may need to learn to identify their feelings. At a morning meeting, ask, *How are you feeling this morning?* "Fine" should not be an acceptable answer. Have each child answer the question one by one. As they speak, list their feelings on the chalkboard. Each child should then be given a paper plate and told to draw his face using any of the emotions listed. The students then use handheld mirrors to look at their faces. Using the paper plates as masks, some children may even want to act out their feelings.

Read *Alexander and the Terrible, Horrible, No Good, Very Bad Day* by Judith Viorst (Atheneum, 1972). Discuss Alexander's feelings throughout the book. Help students understand that feelings are not right or wrong and they can learn to express their feelings without hurting others or losing control.

Solving Conflict

Listening to others is a very important skill in learning to resolve conflicts. Students need to realize how easily words can be misunderstood or the meaning changed by not listening carefully. To do this, play "Gossip," the game in which one person whispers a message in another's ear and that person whispers to the next and so on until the entire group has heard the message. The last person repeats what was heard.

When you compare the first and last messages, the first student will probably reveal that it was not what she said at all. Discuss how these misunderstandings can lead to conflict.

Then talk about some of the peaceful ways to solve conflicts such as:

Talk about it	Share
Take turns	Say "I'm sorry"
Work together	Walk away
Get help	Compromise

Write the ideas down and keep the chart up all year to refer to when conflict arises in the classroom. You may also want to decide on a process to go through when problems occur. For instance, these steps might be helpful:

1. What is the problem?
2. How can you solve it?
3. Is there another solution?
4. Choose the best solution.
5. Just do it.

Role-Playing

Children need to be aware that conflicts will arise and that they are a natural part of life. Here is a strategy that will aid young children in dealing with conflicts with peers. Train the children to use the following sequence, and then have them apply the steps in role-play and actual situations that occur during the school day. Have two children face

each other and make eye contact to ensure active listening. Give these directives to the child who is actively resolving the conflict:

- Look at the other child and say his or her name.
- Express your feelings about the situation. Say "I feel ____ when you ____."
- Tell the other child what you would like to happen.

Recognition

Explain to the students that the Nobel Peace Prize is given to special people who make great efforts to bring peace to the world. Talk about giving peace prizes in your classroom. The award might be special recognition on the bulletin board for a week or a special badge to wear throughout the day. Have the class discuss ways to demonstrate peaceful actions such as counting to 10 when you are upset or angry, using words and not hands to express your frustration, and taking turns when you and a friend want to play different things. Set aside a special time when the students can nominate classmates for peace prizes. Have the child who nominates tell how the nominee demonstrated peaceful actions. Award and give the winners a round of applause.

Sticker and Stamp Rewards

Reward your students' good behavior with individual stamp and sticker books. Give two booklets (one sheet of paper folded in fourths) to each child. Have the child print "My Sticker Book" on the front of one and "My Stamp Book" on the other. That will leave three pages in the book for students to place their rewards, about six to nine stickers or stamps on each page. Use stickers for good grades and rubber stamps for good behavior, returning notes on time, and other responsible behavior. When a stamp book is full, award a coupon book to the child with coupons for a free pencil, a homework pass, a free book, and so on. When a sticker book is full, award the student a special prize.

Behavior Management

Monkey Business

Bring a stuffed gorilla to school and keep it on a shelf in the classroom. When you see someone working very hard, announce that the student does not "monkey around." Let that student have the gorilla on his desk for the day. A checklist will ensure that everyone has the opportunity to have the gorilla as a partner. Students will enjoy the company and work hard to earn the gorilla.

Adding up Points

Use a point system based on group effort to keep discipline in your classroom. The group that gets the most points for the week gets a trip to the treasure chest (filled with inexpensive treats and prizes). Let students choose names for their groups, and keep a list of the group names on the chalkboard. Mark a point for each positive behavior you see.

Paper Punch Motivation

Give each student a die-cut shape every two weeks. (Use seasonal shapes such as pumpkins for fall, trees or stars for Christmas, hearts for February, shamrocks for March, flowers for spring, and so on.) Throughout the day, ask children who are listening well, helping someone, working hard, and so on to make a paper punch on their shapes. After two weeks, count the holes punched on each child's shape. Reward the top three students with paperback books, posters, or other prizes.

That Silly Goldilocks!

Read *Goldilocks and the Three Bears*, retold and illustrated by James Marshall (Puffin, 1998). After reading the book, discuss the manners Goldilocks should have used when visiting the bears' house: knocking and asking permission before going into the house, being careful with the bears' furniture and possessions, and so on. Then have children brainstorm ideas about what good manners Goldilocks should use if she visits their school. Generate a list of manners she would need to follow, such as keeping hands and feet to herself, raising her hand to talk, saying kind things about others, saying "please" and "thank you," and so on. After the brainstorming session, print the ideas in a class book entitled "Good Manners for Goldilocks at School."

Popcorn Party

To incorporate a class celebration into your behavior plan, let your students earn unpopped popcorn kernels for demonstrating positive behaviors. The kernels are then added to a Popcorn Party Jar. When it's full (it should be small enough so that it gets filled fairly often) celebrate by popping the popcorn in an air popper. This provides entertainment as the students will love to watch it pop. Eat popcorn, drink juice, and have fun! This is the perfect no-mess party as well as being a positive reinforcement for good behavior. It's a simple plan, but it works wonderfully.

Positive Notes

To motivate students in reading and writing, write positive notes to them. Tape notes to desktops to be found first thing in the morning. For example: "Jessica, your desk is super clean!" Not only will children's self-esteem increase, but they may soon start leaving notes on your desk.

Jessica, your desk is super clean!

Soothing Music

Bring a portable CD player along with classical and relaxing CDs to school. Every day play soothing music at a volume that allows for soft talking. When the noise level gets too high, tell your students that you can't hear the music. After several months, the number of times the students get too loud will drop dramatically. Now the students will be reminding each other that they can't hear the music. Their attention spans will increase and they are being exposed to classical music. This idea is a winner all around.

Please Stay Seated!

To encourage students to stay seated when required, pass out a piece of candy, a sticker, or some other little treat to each one. If a child chooses to get up at an inappropriate time, she must surrender the treat. Being able to keep the treat to eat or enjoy rewards students who stay seated.

A Well-Mannered Giraffe

Color and cut out the giraffe. Poke a metal fastener through the circles on the neck and body to put him together. Write the poem on the giraffe. Bend the giraffe's neck and make him say "Please," "Thank you," and "Excuse me."

Big or little, short or tall,
Be sure to show good
Manners to all.
Always say, "Please,"
And "Excuse me" too,
And never forget to say
"Thank you."

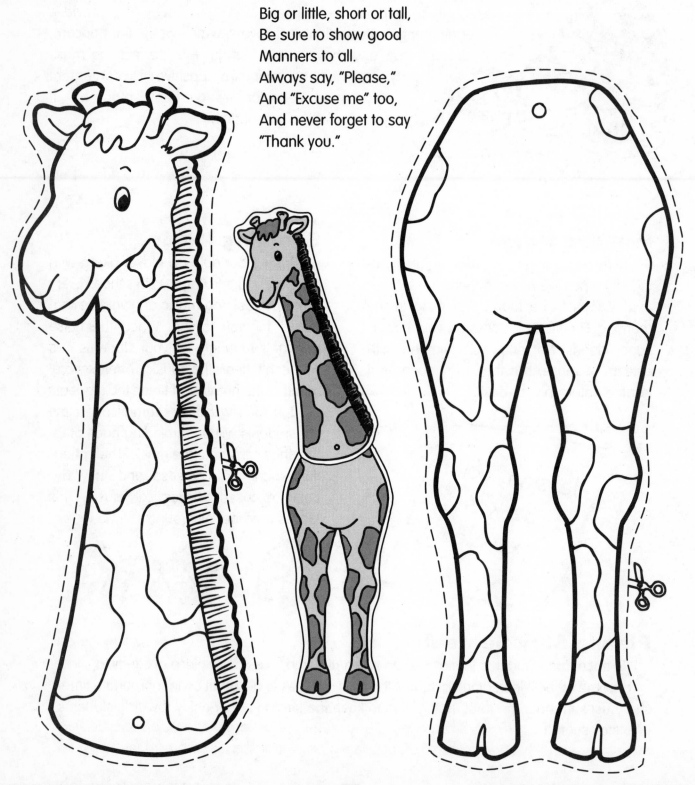

Positive Beginning Sticks

Print your students' names on ice cream or craft sticks, one for each student. When students come into the room in the morning, hand each one a stick with someone else's name on it. When everyone is seated, explain that everyone is going to walk up to the person whose name they have and give that person a compliment to start off the day on a positive note. When the compliments are done, collect all the sticks for the next time.

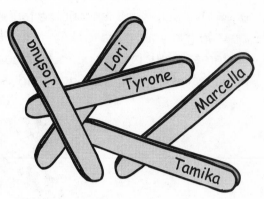

Kindness Counts

Employ this student pledge on the first day of the new school year:

> I will act in such a way that I will be proud of myself and my family will be proud of me, too. I came to school to learn and I will learn something new each day! My actions reflect my concern for others. I will have an awesome day!

After saying the pledge together, find something kind to say to one another. To reinforce the kindness issue, bring a doll to class and draw a large heart on it. Every time someone says something unkind to someone else, pin an X on the doll's heart. The children won't like to see the X's. If that person who said something unkind says something kind to the person who was hurt, remove the X from the doll's heart.

A Responsibility Board

Involve the class in developing a board that reflects commitment to responsible behavior. Have them brainstorm responsible acts such as throwing trash in the trash can, putting supplies away in their proper places, and listening when others are talking. Encourage the children to share the responsible behaviors they have noted.

After identifying specific actions, each child can set a goal for himself that requires responsible behavior. Have each child draw a picture of what she is committed to doing. Title the bulletin board "We Pledge to Act Responsibly." You may want to place a photograph of each child by his drawing. This personalizes the goal setting and motivates the commitment.

Behavior Management

Show-and-Tell Lunch Guests

Get to know older and younger classmates with this fun Show-and-Tell. On a rotating basis one day each week, encourage four or five students to each invite a friend from a different class to join your class for lunch. Just before lunch, introduce the guests. Have your students tell three or four interesting facts about each guest. At lunchtime, designate a special table for host/hostesses and their Show-and-Tell lunch guests.

Pet Show

Make one of your Show-and-Tell times a Pet Show-and-Tell. Assign each child a date and a time slot. For this unique event, invite each child to bring a real or stuffed pet to visit with the classmates. Schedule visits from live pets for early morning or late afternoon times.

Joke of the Day

Primary students love telling jokes. Invite each student to tell a favorite joke during Show-and-Tell. Explain that jokes can be memorized or read aloud. For extra pizzazz, tape-record your joke sessions for Parents' Night. Another fun idea is to choose a different student every week to kick off Monday morning school-wide announcements with a funny story. Compile the jokes to create your own class joke book.

Travel Talk

Give each student a blank 5" x 8" (12.7 cm x 20.3 cm) index card. Invite children to design postcards of favorite vacation spots. Share vacation facts and fantasies on Postcard Show-and-Tell Day.

The Sharing Box

Decorate a shoebox and title it "Sharing Box." Place it in a convenient area in your classroom. Have your students take turns bringing something from home to share. Whoever is sharing must also write something about the shared object. The child could describe the object, tell where it came from, or say why she considers it special. If the child wants the item to be touched, it is placed on top of the paper in the box. If the child doesn't want it to be touched, it is placed under the paper. Pass the shoebox around during an independent study.

A Mystery Bag

Make a small drawstring fabric bag. Make a class set of "spy glasses" or magnifying glasses cut out of paper. Write a different student's name on each spy glass. Randomly choose a Number One Detective each week. Let him take home the fabric Mystery Bag.

Tuck inside the bag a parent note explaining that the child is to choose an object from home to fit in the bag and return the bag to school during the week. Explain that the family is to help the child write two or three sentences telling about the object, but not naming it.

When the Number One Detective returns the bag to school, have him read aloud the sentences. Have the rest of the class try to guess what's inside the Mystery Bag. What a great way to get children sharing orally and thinking creatively.

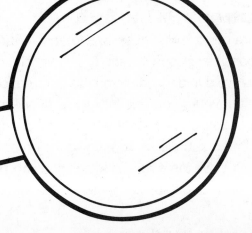

Planning for a Substitute

Sub Assist for Special Subs

Prepare a portfolio for the substitute teacher, including these important items:

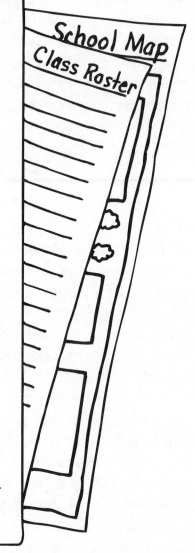

- A school map with room numbers marked
- Your teaching schedule
- Your duty and special schedule
- A monthly school calendar for school programs
- The name and location of another teacher who is familiar with you and your students
- A class roster with notes listing names of students who are good assistants and notes about students' nicknames (Jon instead of Jonathan, Sophia instead of Tien Su)
- General routines and daily sequences (pledge to the flag, song, and so on)
- The custodian's name and location (a great help to the sub if a child gets sick or someone spills something)
- Location of the office intercom or buzzer and the secretary's name
- A list of songs and words that your students enjoy (nursery rhymes, etc.)
- A list of movement activities with rules or words
- Instructions and cards for memory games
- Copies of favorite books to read
- A large empty envelope for the sub to insert homework or notes from students and comments to you

Solutions for a Sub

Here are a few suggestions to ensure that your sub has a great day:

If possible, phone the sub to go over class rules and possible problem areas. If this isn't possible, leave a folder containing this information. Also include in the folder recess and lunch times and when you go outside for recess duty. Provide some activity sheets for time fillers.

Leave lesson plans out where they can be easily found. If it's a planned absence, tell students that a sub will be coming so they aren't surprised (or even scared).

Don't leave ten pages of instructions and don't expect everything to be completed. It's tough being a sub and it takes a while for the sub and the students to get to know one another.

A Great Day for the Sub

Why not plan ahead so that your sub can come into your classroom and have a great day? Of course, it's a must to leave detailed plans for your sub, including an outline of the day listed in blocks of time. As a special treat, leave a large box labeled "Substitute Station." This box should contain extra worksheets and games, several joke and riddle books, as well as a general list of opening duties and dismissal procedures.

Helpful Hints for Subs

- Refer to the substitute as a "guest teacher." That way the children will consider her a guest for the day rather than someone who is substituting for you.
- Make nametags for students ahead of time that they will know to put on when a substitute is in the room.
- Leave a clean coffee cup, a tea bag or hot chocolate mix, and a granola bar for the sub to enjoy during his or her break.
- If you are the sub, take a "magic teacher's bag" to class. Fill it with treats, videos, and books. Every so often during the day, pull a treat out of the bag and have a "bag break."
- If you are the sub, give out I.C.U. (I See You) awards to students who display cooperative behaviors throughout the day. First, the student earns an I.C.U. card and then you stamp it each time you observe a positive behavior. Let the returning teacher know who earned the awards.

Panoramic Pictures

Besides having a classroom set of nametags ready for your students to wear whenever you need a substitute, display a panoramic class picture and place one inside the substitute folder. Purchase a disposable panoramic camera (share the cost with other teachers who wish to use the camera). Have the students line up in rows for the two snapshots. After your photographs are developed, place small labels or dot stickers by each child and write the appropriate child's name on each label.

Get-to-Know-You Games for the Sub

Pass the Ball

Have the students sit in a circle. Tell them that they are going to pass a ball around the circle while the music is playing. When the music stops, the child holding the ball must say his name. Continue the game until all the students have said their names.

Guess the Groups

Have the students sit in a group a couple of feet away from you. Decide on two classifications like "children wearing green" and "children not wearing green." Do not tell the students how you intend to group them. Choose one student for each criterion and ask each child to stand in front of the group. Continue choosing until you have three children in each group. Ask the rest of the class to guess how you are grouping the students. If no one answers correctly, continue placing children in each group. Ask the rest of the class to guess how you are grouping the students. If no one answers correctly, continue placing children in each group. When someone guesses correctly, she can choose the next classification, whisper it in your ear, and start the process again.

What I Like

Have everyone sit in a circle. Ask a simple question that can be answered with "My name is ___ and I like ___." For example, *What's your name and what's your favorite book?* Or *What's your name and what's your favorite thing to do at school?* Go around the circle and have each child say his name and answer the question. Repeat the child's name and the answer. By the time everyone has responded, you'll have a good idea of who everyone is!

What's your name and what's your favorite book?

What's your name and what's your favorite thing to do at school?

Language Arts

Milk Carton Begins with M

Young children need practice listening for the beginning sounds of words, but it can be tiresome to use the same worksheets and oral reviews over and over. Have students wash half-pint milk cartons and let them dry for a day. Instruct them to cut apart their worksheets, picking out the words that begin with the same sound as "milk." Ask them to put these **m** words inside their milk cartons. Provide old magazines from which they may cut more **m** words and pictures to put in their milk cartons. Before class is over, staple the cartons shut. Encourage the children to take them home and quiz their parents on what **m** things might be in the cartons before opening them.

Hands-On Letter Sounds

As you work on identifying letters and their sounds, create a mobile for each letter. Glue two cards with the same letter on them back-to-back over the neck of a wire clothes hanger. Collect four or five items beginning with the sound of that letter and hang them from the clothes hanger with various lengths of yarn.

Silly Sentences

Divide the class into three groups. Each student in Group 1 chooses a color name and keeps it a secret. Each child in Group 2 chooses an animal, and each child in Group 3 chooses a place. Call on a child from each group at random to come to the front of the room and share her word. The children must try to make a sentence using all three words (the color, the animal, and the place). Some silly sentences will result. (Example: The purple kangaroo went to the grocery store.) After a few weeks of this kind of oral sharing, have students write down some of their sentences and illustrate them for a class big book.

Language Arts

Edible Punctuation

To introduce punctuation, hand out these food items to represent punctuation marks.

- Small marshmallow— period
- Pretzel stick—exclamation point
- Elbow macaroni—question mark

Have students write sentences, gluing a food punctuation mark at the end of each. They'll never forget punctuation marks again.

Lunch Menu Reading and Writing

Have individual students spell aloud the items found on the day's lunch menu as a student or teacher writes them on the chalkboard. Then have volunteers read the list aloud. Ask questions about the menu, such as: What word on the menu begins with the same sound as the word "chair"? What word would we have if we changed the "p" in "pickle" to a "t"?

Hidden Letters

Play this game with young students to help them practice spelling their names. First, hide letter cards throughout the room. Then ask children to search for the letters, collecting only those that appear in their own names. After the children collect all the letters that spell each of their names, place their letters in individual envelopes. Let the children use their letters to practice spelling their names.

Linking Word Parts

Reinforce beginning blends by having students link word parts. Cut a large supply of 3" x 12" (7.6 cm x 30.5 cm) construction paper strips. On each strip, print a beginning blend (such as **sh, th, ch**, and so on). Then cut additional strips of different colors. Hand out these strips to students. Have them print word parts that can be added to the beginning blends to make words. Have each student say the word part, then the entire word as his link is fastened to the beginning blend link of the word chain.

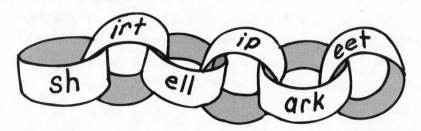

Hands-On Word Ring

Cut 3" x 5" (7.6 cm x 12.7 cm) cards in half and punch a hole in each one. Use a marker to print a vocabulary word on each one. Print a student's name on one card. Hook the cards together with a metal ring. Make a set for each student. Students can use their word rings in a variety of ways, alone or with a partner: removing the words from the ring and making sentences, putting the words in alphabetical order on their desks, sorting out the long vowel words, short vowel words, blend words, rhyming words, and word families.

Letter Vests

To make a letter vest, each student will need:
- a large, brown paper grocery bag
- scissors
- crayons

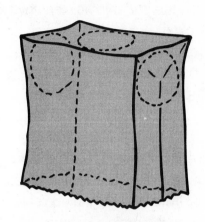

Directions:
1. Print the letter you're studying on the front of the vest.
2. Print words and draw pictures that begin with the featured letter. Cut armholes, a neck hole, and a front slit, as shown.
3. Put on the vest and march around the room saying the letter and words that begin with that letter.

We Like Books!

Read *I Like Books* by Anthony Browne (Random House, 1997) to your class. In this book, a sweet-faced chimp likes all kinds of books—funny books, scary books, comic books, coloring books, books about monsters, and books about space.

After reading this charming book, conduct a poll among your students. Cut a book cover silhouette from colored paper for each student. Have students write the title and author of their favorite book on the cutouts. Then have each one draw colorful illustrations of her favorite part of the book on white paper that can be glued to the cutout cover. Ask each student to give a brief book talk about the book he selected. Mount the illustrated book cutouts on the bulletin board under the caption "We Like Books!"

Language Arts

Flip Phonics

To make a flip sheet, each student will need:

- one 12" x 18" (30.5 cm x 20.3 cm) sheet of construction paper
- scissors
- crayons

Directions:

1. Fold the paper in half lengthwise.
2. Make five cuts, three inches apart, from the edge of the paper to the fold line as shown. This will form six flaps.
3. On the front side of each flap, print a beginning sound, vowel sound, or blend.
4. Under each flap, draw a picture to illustrate the designated sound.
5. When the project is done, the student can flip up the flaps to review the sounds and their illustrations.

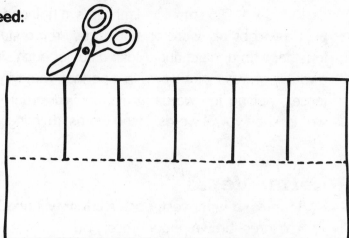

Pet Pictures

To encourage students to write, bring a pet to school or schedule a day for each student to bring in a pet from home. Take pictures of students with the pet using a camcorder or instant camera. Insert the photos into a word processing document so students can write computer stories about their own pets. You may prefer to print the pictures using a color printer, glue them on sheets of paper, and have students glue or write handwritten stories below.

Follow a Raindrop

Read *Follow a Raindrop: The Water Cycle* by Elsie Ward (Scholastic, 2000) to introduce the water cycle to your students. After reading this story aloud, ask your students to imagine that they are raindrops. Then have them write stories about their adventures around the world.

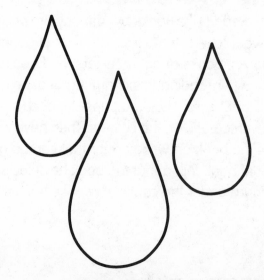

Sunny Words

On a bright, sunny day, ask students to list all the words they can that include the word sun. Begin with: *sunup*, *sundown*, *sunset*, *sunrise*.

Continuous Alphabet

Discover this super-quick way to practice cursive writing. Give your students three minutes to write the entire alphabet as many times as possible. Have them write without raising their pencils from the paper. The only lifts accepted are to dot the *i* and *j*, or to cross the *t* and *x*. This simple activity focuses on letter formation without spelling.

abcdefghijklmnopq

Words with Personality

Did you know that words have personalities? Some are pleasant, and some are unpleasant. Have students list all the words that are pleasing to them. Begin with *jolly*, *happy*, and *smiling*. Then they list words that are unpleasant to them. Begin with *mean*, *grumpy*, and *ugly*.

Colorful Compounds

Many compound words include color words. Ask students to list as many colorful compound words as they can. Begin with *blueberry*, *black-bird*, and *greenhouse*.

Menu Magic

Ask restaurant managers for samples of their menus. Take the menus to school and have your class write the selections in alphabetical order. They may also write their favorite dishes in order.

Alphabet Scavenger Hunt

A fun homework assignment to help teach beginning letter sounds is a modified scavenger hunt. Ask students and their families to locate in their homes five items that begin with the assigned letter. Then, have students draw and label each item. Ask them to share their lists with each other. Make a book to take home and share with their families. Compile the individual lists into class charts. Have students take turns spelling and reading the words they recognize.

Language Arts

Name Game

Have students look through magazines or catalogs to find pictures of people with expressive facial or body language. Have children create a list of names that seem to match the spirit or attitude of each picture. Or help the children develop a list of names for characters they would like to write about. Then have them draw or search for pictures of people who fit the names.

Place Settings

Physically mapping out a story setting on a piece of unlined paper is a wonderful way to help students develop a sense of place. It can also lead to a better understanding of the relationship between the setting and the characters. First, have children think of a setting that interests them, such as an apartment complex, a desert, a space station, or a ghost town. Then encourage children to include all of the landmarks that might be found in this setting or might be important to a story that occurs there. Have them think carefully about the arrangement of these landmarks, and the distance between them. Make sure that they label the landmarks clearly, so the map is understandable to the rest of the group.

Word Collage

Have students make a collage of drawings or magazine pictures based on an assigned theme of their own choice. Then help them think of words that describe the pictures included in their work. You might encourage them to locate suitable words in the magazines they have used, or to refer to a dictionary. Have them incorporate their words into their collages.

First or Last?

Read and reread nursery rhymes to your students to help them identify first and last in a sequence of events. Begin by reading "Hickory, Dickory, Dock."

Hickory, dickory, dock!
The mouse ran up the clock!
The clock struck one,
The mouse ran down,
Hickory, dickory, dock!

Ask children to listen as you reread the rhyme for what happens first (the mouse ran up the clock). Ask children to listen for what happens last as you read the rhyme again (the mouse ran down). Reread the rhyme once more, having children chant the first and last lines with you. Continue to practice first and last with these Mother Goose rhymes:

"Little Miss Muffett"
"Jack and Jill"
"The Cat and the Fiddle"
"Little Jack Horner"
"To Market, to Market"
"This Little Pig Went to Market"

Hand each student a piece of 5" (13.9 cm) drawing paper. Instruct the class to fold the paper in half and draw what happened first in the nursery rhyme in one section and what happened last in the other section. Then have them label the sections "first" and "last."

ABC Book

Here's a simple, effective homework idea for young children who are learning the alphabet. On a 9" x 12" (22.8 cm x 30.5 cm) piece of newsprint, each student traces around a cardboard uppercase letter pattern and around a lowercase pattern of the same letter. Then the student takes the paper home to color the letters. There, the child also cuts out matching letters from newspaper headlines and pictures beginning with that letter to paste on the page.

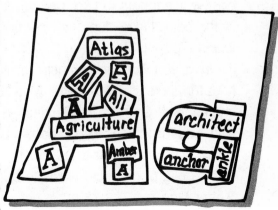

The page is returned to school and kept until all 26 pages have been completed. Then the students sequence the letters to make an ABC book and add a special cover. Finally, they take the completed books home to share with their families.

Language Arts

Cupcake Creatures

Here's a delicious writing idea that your students will love. Prepare a plain cupcake for each student in the class. Set up a table where children can decorate their cupcakes with frosting, small pretzels, colored sprinkles, raisins, marshmallows, chocolate chips, and candy corn.

Have two or three students at a time visit the decorating center and create a cupcake creature. Then children take their cupcakes back to their desks and write stories about them. Encourage children to use interesting adjectives to describe their creatures.

You may wish to snap a photograph of each child holding his cupcake before he enjoys eating his snack. Display pictures of the yummy creatures and the stories on a bulletin board.

Favorite Food

Cut strips of paper. On each strip, write the name of a food that children especially like (popcorn, pizza, ice cream, spaghetti). Place the strips in a container and have each child choose one. Have students to pretend they have become that food and write about their experiences.

For example, if pizza is chosen, have students write about how it feels to be rolled into a ball, kneaded, rolled out flat, dressed in gooey toppings, and heated to a high temperature.

Letter Man

Your students will have fun learning letter names with this activity. Draw a "Letter Man" on the chalkboard using different letters of the alphabet. Ask students to suggest which letters to use for various parts of the body. Have students copy the Letter Man on paper.

In a variation of this activity, children take turns creating the "Letter Man" on the chalkboard. Each child identifies a letter and adds it to the "Letter Man." You can also ask your students to use a letter taken from a pile of alphabet cards to build the "Letter Man."

Stuffed Animals Make for Great Writing

Stuffed animals are great for stimulating writing. Bring a large stuffed animal to class for a month. Let the class name the animal and spend some time talking about him. Beginning with his name, create a word web showing his characteristics. In the web, include his color, size, food preferences, and other attributes. After your discussion, encourage your students to write short stories about your animal. The next month, begin again with a new stuffed animal.

Class Portrait Stories

Make a photocopy of your class group photograph for each student. Have each child mount the portrait on the upper portion of a sheet of writing paper. Then have students write a creative story about the picture. As an alternative springtime activity, cut the portrait apart to obtain individual pictures. These can be mounted in drawings of spring flowers. Then have students write about these unique gardens.

Inspire Writing with Pictures

Use pictures that tell part of a story to inspire creative writing. Popular coloring books are a great source of such pictures. Choose a few action pictures to color and laminate. Display them and watch your young authors eagerly begin to write.

Writing Thank-You Notes

When teaching students how to write thank-you notes, first have them practice on school paper. Working together, make corrections in spelling, grammar, and indentations. The next day, give each student a piece of stationery on which to rewrite her or his thank-you note. Use lined stationery for younger students.

Letters to Authors

Collect addresses of authors and illustrators. Then copy the addresses and place them in the back of books by those authors and illustrators. This will stimulate your students to write letters to their favorite authors and illustrators after they have read a book.

Language Arts

Syllable Name Chart

Use student names to reinforce syllables. Post a chart on a classroom wall. Write category headings that identify the number of syllables in a child's name. When students have free time, they write their names under the correct heading.

One	Two	Three
Anne	Stacy	Emily
Tom	Billy	
Ben		

Hands-On Spelling

Have three or four students at a time go to a spelling center to work on the week's spelling words and sentences. Provide magnetic letters, letter tiles, letter stamps, and interlocking letter puzzle pieces, and have the children rotate through the activities during the 30 minutes they are at the center. Once in while, you may also want to put out sponge letters and paint for the students to use. Encourage your students to visit this center at least once a week. Watch the spelling improve.

Story Folders

Gather interesting pictures from magazines or calendars for this creative writing center. Glue each picture inside a file folder. Write a motivating question under each picture. Across from the picture, list several words that the students might need to write about the picture and to answer the question. Be sure to include several nouns, verbs, adjectives, and adverbs. Laminate each folder for durability, and if you wish, give each folder a title or a number. Place the folders in a file box at the center. Have story paper, pencils, and crayons available. The students choose a folder and then write a story about the picture.

Nature Alphabet

On your next nature hike, provide each student with a lunch bag that has several letters of the alphabet printed on the front. Tell the students that each child's job is to find one item in nature that begins with each individual letter and collect it in his bag. (Examples: r—rock, l—leaf, and w—weed.) You may have to repeat letters. Remind the children to be safe and careful with what they pick up—no insects, bugs, and other living things.

When you return to class, have each student share what she or he has found, naming each letter and sound.

Colors of the Rainbow

Create a multicolored chart using the rainbow colors. Print the name of a color on each section. Have students match color stripes with the color words printed on them to the larger multicolor chart. Point out that not only do the colors match, but the words also correspond. As the words become more familiar, use white cards with color words printed on them to do this activity. Finally, have students match the words to a multicolored chart that is not labeled with color words. This is a super activity to introduce color sight words, reinforce knowledge, and provide a nice evaluation as well.

Something Is Missing

Emphasize the importance of vowels in words with this simple activity. Divide the class into groups of four or five students. Provide each group with a paper lunch bag containing 10 to 12 letter cards, each with a different consonant. Leave out all the vowels. Ask the groups to spell as many words as they can using their letter cards. They will soon discover that without vowels, the task is impossible. Then provide vowel cards for each group and challenge the students again to form words. Have groups share some of the words they made.

Hop and Spell

Movement is a valuable phonics reinforcement tool because it's fun and it provides an experience that encourages thinking in a different way. List on a chart some of the word families the students have been studying. Also write each letter of the alphabet with a marker on a separate sheet of paper. Place the letters close together on the floor in random order. Ask a student to think of a word that could be made from a word family on the chart and to hop from one letter to another to spell the word. The rest of the students must watch carefully and guess the word that is being spelled. Because this activity requires that children track the path of the word, hold it in their mind, and then visualize the word, it strengthens visual memory.

Language Arts

Little Red Hen Rhymes

After sharing the book *The Little Red Hen* retold by Harriet Ziefert (Puffin, 1995), ask your students which words they remember from the story. List these words on the chalkboard. After writing several words, challenge the students to come up with a rhyming word for each word listed, as shown here:

cat   flat
goose   loose
vain   rain
lazy   crazy
bread   red

Demonstrate how to use a pair of the rhyming words to create a couplet poem, such as the following:

The dog was so lazy,
He drove us all crazy!

Challenge the students to create their own couplet poems using pairs of rhyming words. Let the students illustrate their poems and share them with the class. You may even want to compile the poems into a class book so the students can take turns taking it home to share the red hen word play with their families.

Color Parade

Use crayons to introduce young children to alphabetical order. First, review the alphabet. Emphasize to the children that the letters are arranged in a specific order. Next, give each child a box of eight crayons. Then tell the children that their challenge is to place the crayons in alphabetical order by color name. Let the children work independently or do this as a whole class activity. Post an alphabet wall chart for reference.

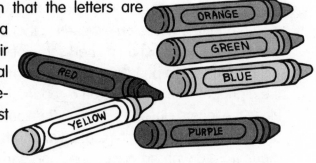

Alphabet Circle Game

Help improve your students' phonics skills as well as alphabetical order with this game. Have the students sit in a circle. Choose one student to start. This student walks around the outside of the circle saying the alphabet in order. At any letter, he gently taps another student on the shoulder. The student who is tapped must make the sound of the letter and says a word that begins with that letter. If her response is correct, these two students switch roles. If the response is incorrect, the student who did the tapping chooses another student to answer.

The ABCs of the School Year

Reinforce alphabetical order by keeping a running list on chart paper of classroom projects, special events, field trips, visitors, curriculum studies, etc., in alphabetical order. Make a large wall chart with the letters of the alphabet printed vertically along the left side of the paper. Each time you want to record something that pertains to the class, list it beside the appropriate letter. The last week of school review the alphabetical list with your students so they can enjoy recapping their eventful school year.

Edible Alphabet

Introduce alphabetical order to younger children and promote good nutrition at the same time. Provide a variety of fresh fruits and vegetables such as pears, apples, oranges, grapes, lettuce, carrots, and zucchini. Print on an index card the initial letter of each food and place the card next to the food item. Talk about a special way to arrange the food items. Use an alphabet wall display and the "ABC Song" as a reference. Together as a class, place the foods in alphabetical order from left to right. When this activity is completed, let the children prepare a salad for a tasty snack.

ABC Order

Whenever you collect completed papers from your students, collect them in alphabetical order by the first name of each student. This reinforces alphabetical order, reviews the names of the students for the class, and arranges the papers in a convenient way to record in your grade book. It's a handy way to note who was absent or who didn't complete the work. Also, when your students line up for an activity, have them line up in alphabetical order (first practice by first names and then by last names). Your students may get so good at alphabetical order that they can line up backwards, starting with Z.

Walking Words

This is a buddy game that can be played when students have free time. Print words on paper foot shapes and place them on the floor. You can use as many as you'd like. Tell students to walk through the feet and pick up all the nouns. You may alter the activity by telling students to pick up the pronouns, adjectives, or verbs.

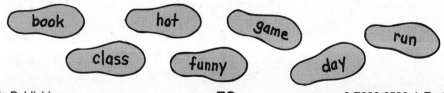

An ABC Hike

Name _____

Cut and paste the letters in the right places.

© McGraw-Hill Children's Publishing

0-7682-2526-4 *Fast Ideas for Busy Teachers*

Short Vowels

Name _____

1. Color green: three pictures that have the short **o** sound as in **top**.
2. Color red: two pictures that have the short **a** sound as in **hat**.
3. Color blue: four pictures that have the short **e** sound as in **hen**.
4. Color orange: three pictures that have the short **u** sound as in **bug**.

Bright Lights

Name _____

Read the word on each bulb. Use a yellow crayon to color the light bulbs with the **long i** sound. The **long i** sounds like the **i** in **light**.

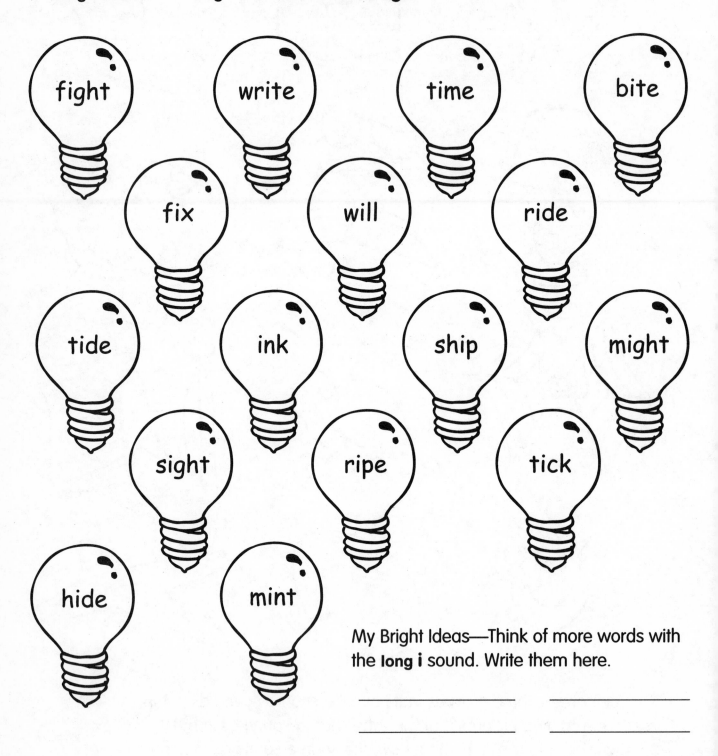

fight   write   time   bite

fix   will   ride

tide   ink   ship   might

sight   ripe   tick

hide   mint

My Bright Ideas—Think of more words with the **long i** sound. Write them here.

_____   _____

_____   _____

© McGraw-Hill Children's Publishing   0-7682-2526-4 *Fast Ideas for Busy Teachers*

Math

What Is a Million?

A million can be a number beyond the grasp of young students. Read aloud the book *If You Made a Million* by David Schwartz and Steven Kellogg (Scott Foresman, 1994). Your class may enjoy collecting a million of something, such as inches of yarn. Encourage students to bring skeins of yarn to class. Measure the number of yards in each skein and convert it to inches. Let students wind the yarn into a giant yarn ball. The average skein contains about 160 yards, so it takes about 174 skeins to total a million inches. Another good book to read is *Millions of Cats* by Wanda Gag (Paper Star, 1996).

It you're not ready to tackle a million, try this counting project with your students. Have each student make ten sets of their ten fingerprints on a sheet of paper. Instruct them to use a marker to add ears, whiskers, and tails to the fingerprints to make them look like cats. Hang all the cats on the bulletin board with the caption "Hundred of Cats! Thousands of Cats!" Discuss how many of these sheets it would take to total one million cats.

Egg Counting Fun

Write numbers 1 to 12 on the side of plastic eggs with a permanent black marker. Write the same numbers on the bottoms of the cups in an egg carton. Have students match each egg to its correct slot. You may also put the corresponding number of jellybeans in each egg cup for a different game and an added surprise treat.

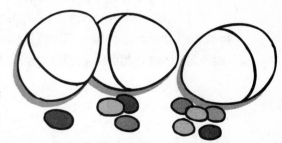

How Many Buttons?

Explain to children that you are going to have a class count of buttons on shirts, blouses, and jackets. Ask each child to stand in front of the class while everyone looks carefully to see if she has any buttons, and if so, to count them. Print the number of buttons on the chalkboard and draw a small circle for each button. Some children will have several buttons; others will have none. When each child's buttons have been counted and put on the board, print an addition problem on the board to reflect the numbers of buttons. Then have the class count the button circles on the board to come up with the total number.

Math

Counting Cookies

To reinforce students' math skills, use the following idea. Fill a jar with cookies and let students estimate how many are in the jar. Present the winner with the contents of the cookie jar for a prize. List various kinds of cookies on the board and let students vote for their favorites. Make a bar graph to show the results.

Shamrock Hunt

Hide small green paper shamrocks around the room. (Hide approximately five for each child.) Give each child an envelope in which to keep the shamrocks he finds. You may want to let students take turns hunting to make sure each one finds at least a couple of shamrocks.

When all the shamrocks have been found, have the children count theirs. Print each child's name on the chalkboard next to her number of shamrocks. Then ask each child to choose a buddy. Have the buddies add their shamrocks together. Print addition problems on the board to reflect these numbers. Then have the children change buddies. Continue until you have several different addition problems on the board.

Number Puzzles

To celebrate the 100th day of school, provide each student with a hundreds chart to cut into puzzle pieces. (Each piece should have at least six numbers.) Then let children try to put the pieces back together to re-create the original hundreds chart. After a child completes his puzzle, suggest trading with another student.

It's best to use black and white copies of the chart so students must rely only on the numbers rather than matching colors.

Patterned Fruit Ring Cereal Necklaces

Distribute a cup of fruit ring cereal to each student. Also give each student a 16" (40.6 cm) piece of yarn. After studying patterning, each child constructs a necklace choosing a pattern of her choice. They love eating the extras.

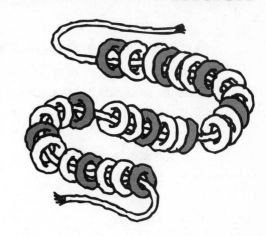

Popcorn Math

Give each student a small plastic bag with 12 paper popcorn shapes in it. Have students number the popcorn shapes from 1 to 9. On the remaining three shapes, they should print a minus sign, a plus sign, and an equal sign. Provide them with popped corn in paper coffee filters. To practice math skills, the student draws two numbered popcorn shapes from the bag and lays them on the desk, using the plus or minus shape and the equal sign to create an addition or subtraction problem. To solve the problem, the student places the correct number of real popcorn pieces after the equal sign. You may want to have students work in pairs on this activity to test each others' math skills.

Numbering Nuts

Bring a bag of nuts or acorns to class. Print several addition and subtraction problems on the board. Let students lay out the nuts in a variety of ways to solve the problems.

Jellybean Estimating

Provide students with different-sized containers (thimble, baby food jars, small cups, and so on). Students estimate how many jellybeans each container holds; then fill and count. How do the results compare to their guesses?

Math

Apple Tree Addition

Before class, spray paint dried lima beans red, yellow, and green. Prepare apple tree patterns for students to trace, or cut out trees for younger children. Use green construction paper for the treetops and brown construction paper for the trunks.

Each student will need:
- pencil
- green and brown construction paper
- scissors
- dark green marker or crayon
- lima beans (2–3 colors)
- glue

Directions:
1. Students trace and cut the treetop from green paper and the trunk from brown paper.
2. After they glue the two pieces together, students use a green marker or crayon to draw leaves on the tree where they will put apples.
3. Students glue colored lima beans to the tree for apples.

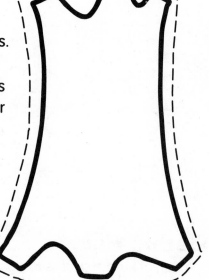

When the trees are done and the glue is dry, have students write simple addition problems to tell about the apples on their trees (7 green apples + 3 red apples = 10 apples).

Edible Estimation

Give each child a graham cracker square. Have them estimate how many miniature marshmallows will fit on the cracker. Record this number; then have the class fill the surface of their crackers with marshmallows, count them, and record this number next to their estimates. They may then eat the marshmallows. Repeat with raisins, square-shaped cereal, pretzels, or any small food item. Notice how the estimates become more accurate by the second try.

Join the Lineup

This number-sequencing activity is sure to score with your students. Copy the football jersey below for each student. Number the jerseys in sequential order. Hand out the jerseys randomly to students. Challenge the children to line up so that the numbers are in numerical order. Then collect and redistribute the jerseys for another round of practice.

For variation, number the jerseys with even/odd numbers, numbers ranging from 1 to 100, or with multiples of 5. Your students will be eager to join the lineup of sequencing all-stars.

Watermelon Count

Name _____

Count the seeds in the watermelon slices. Write on each slice how many seeds it has. Then draw lines to connect the slices that are alike.

Number Words

Name _____

Solve each number fact. Write the answer in word form in the correct place in the crossword puzzle.

ACROSS
1. $2 + 2 =$ _____
2. $9 - 2 =$ _____
4. $4 + 4 =$ _____
6. $6 + 4 =$ _____
7. $0 + 1 =$ _____

DOWN
1. $6 - 1 =$ _____
2. $3 + 3 =$ _____
3. $7 + 2 =$ _____
5. $7 - 4 =$ _____
6. $10 - 8 =$ _____

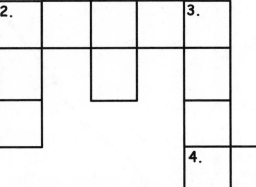

© McGraw-Hill Children's Publishing   0-7682-2526-4 *Fast Ideas for Busy Teachers*

Starfish Estimating

Give each student a copy of the starfish below and a bag of ring-shaped cereal. Have them write a number on their pages to show how many rings they estimate it will take to cover the starfish. Then have them glue the cereal on the starfish, completely covering the shape. When they're done, ask students to count the cereal pieces and compare the actual number with their estimates.

Toy Shopping

Name _____

Read the color words. Match them to the correct amount of money. Add the color values to find the price of each toy.

Color Code: red = 2 cents   yellow = 3 cents
                  blue = 5 cents   black = 1 cent

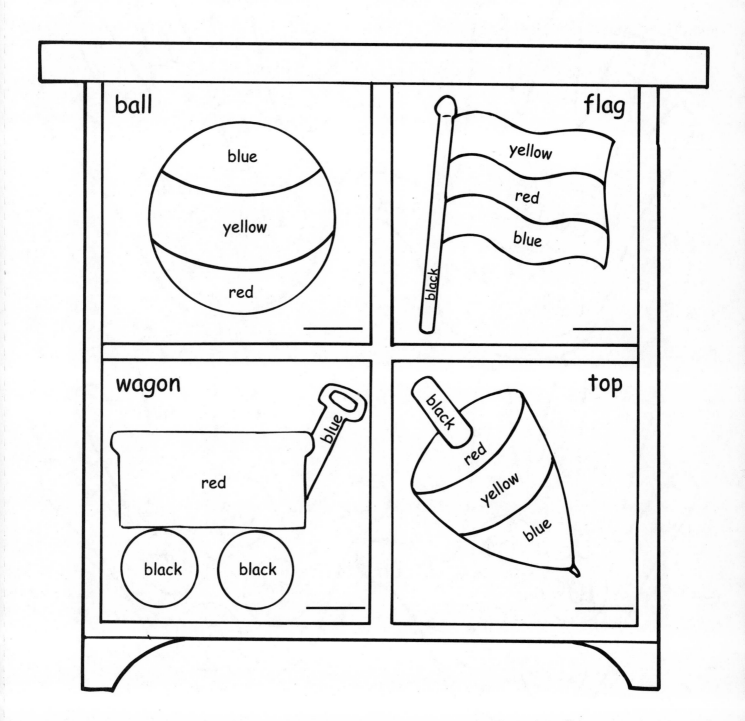

© McGraw-Hill Children's Publishing

0-7682-2526-4 *Fast Ideas for Busy Teachers*

Lunch Money

Name _____

Add the coins each student spent for lunch.

Who spent the most money? _____
Who spent the least money? _____

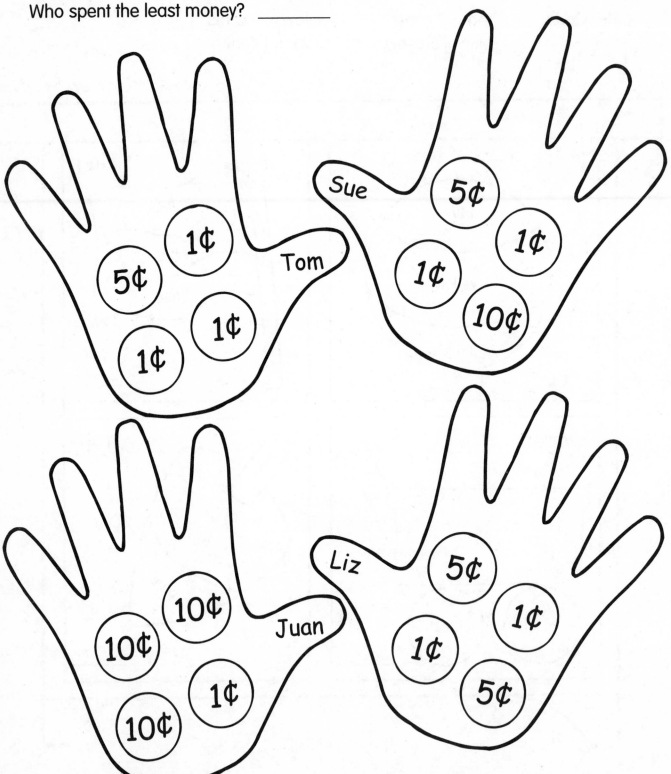

© McGraw-Hill Children's Publishing

0-7682-2526-4 *Fast Ideas for Busy Teachers*

Spring Bouquet

Name _____

In the spring, the woods and fields are full of wild flowers.
Use the color/number key to color the bouquet.

1—yellow   2—purple   3—green   4—blue   5—orange

Take time to smell the flowers.

© McGraw-Hill Children's Publishing

0-7682-2526-4 Fast Ideas for Busy Teachers

Calling All Krill!

Name _____

Add or subtract. Draw a line from the problem to the correct answer on the krill.

I just love to eat krill! Krill is like shrimp!

8 +4	12 −7	9 +3	5 +4
10 −3	6 +4	9 +2	12 −8
11 −9	12 −9	6 +6	11 −5

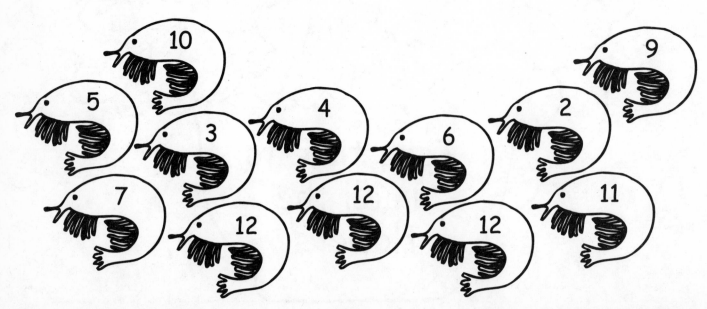

10   5   3   4   6   2   9   7   12   12   12   11

© McGraw-Hill Children's Publishing

0-7682-2526-4 *Fast Ideas for Busy Teachers*

Spin the Sums

Name _____

Cut apart the bug counters. Use them to solve the problems.

$$\begin{array}{r} 3 \\ +5 \\ \hline \end{array}$$

$$\begin{array}{r} 4 \\ +4 \\ \hline \end{array}$$

$$\begin{array}{r} 4 \\ +3 \\ \hline \end{array}$$

$$\begin{array}{r} 7 \\ +2 \\ \hline \end{array}$$

$$\begin{array}{r} 9 \\ +1 \\ \hline \end{array}$$

$$\begin{array}{r} 2 \\ +8 \\ \hline \end{array}$$

$$\begin{array}{r} 6 \\ +3 \\ \hline \end{array}$$

$$\begin{array}{r} 2 \\ +4 \\ \hline \end{array}$$

$$\begin{array}{r} 5 \\ +4 \\ \hline \end{array}$$

$$\begin{array}{r} 1 \\ +5 \\ \hline \end{array}$$

© McGraw-Hill Children's Publishing

0-7682-2526-4 *Fast Ideas for Busy Teachers*

Drip, Drop Math

Name _____

Add the numbers. Then color the raindrops with **even** answers **light blue**. Color the **odd** number raindrops **dark blue**.

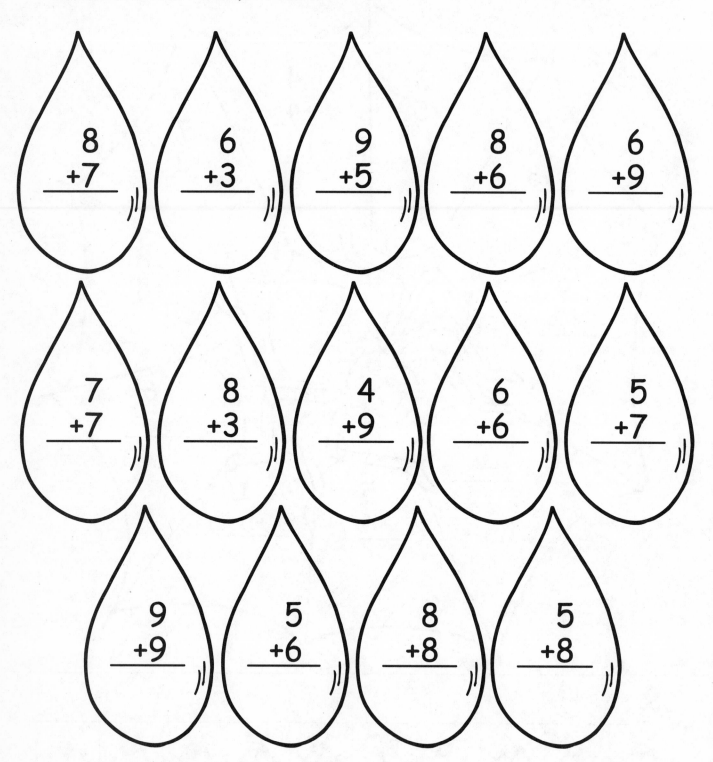

$$8 + 7$$

$$6 + 3$$

$$9 + 5$$

$$8 + 6$$

$$6 + 9$$

$$7 + 7$$

$$8 + 3$$

$$4 + 9$$

$$6 + 6$$

$$5 + 7$$

$$9 + 9$$

$$5 + 6$$

$$8 + 8$$

$$5 + 8$$

Science

An Amphibian's Life Cycle

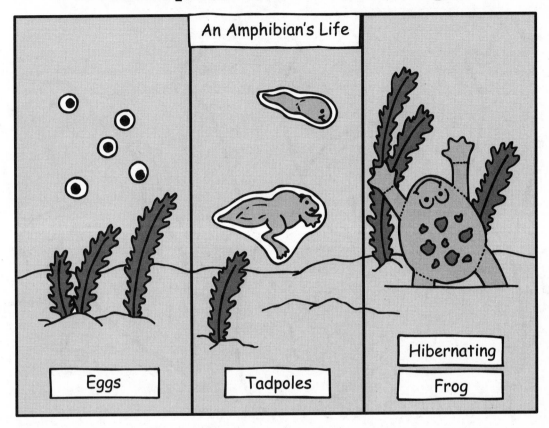

1. Section a 12" x 18" (30.4 cm x 45.7 cm) sheet of white paper into thirds.

2. Have students color the bottom section of each third like the bottom of a pond; and the top section like the water. Have them include plants in the scene.

3. Stick white paper reinforcement circles in the water in the first section. Color the centers black to make them look like eggs.

4. Color and cut out tadpole shapes from the patterns on page 78. Glue them in the water in the center section of the scene.

5. Cut a slit in the bottom of the pond (the mud) in the third section. Attach an envelope to the back of the sheet behind the slit.

6. Color and cut out a frog pattern from page 78. Let the frog swim around in the pond for a while, then fold it up and place it in the slit in the scene to hibernate for the winter.

7. Label the sections as shown above.

An Amphibian's Life Cycle Patterns

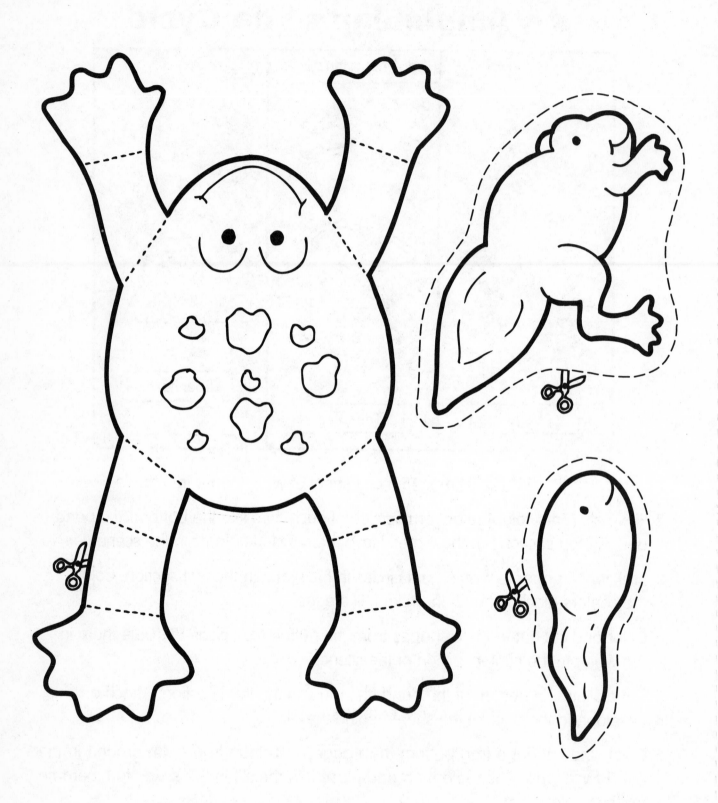

Sing a Song of Cycles

Keep the water cycle fresh in your students' minds with this song.

(Tune: "Twinkle, Twinkle Little Star")

Water falling from the sky,
Falling from the clouds up high.
Pretty soon the sun will come
Warming you, then up you'll run
Back into the sky again,
The water cycle never ends!

Rainbow Adventures

Explain to your class that a rainbow is actually sunlight passing through tiny raindrops. The water causes sunlight to separate, so that we can see all the colors that make up light. The color bands of a rainbow are always in the same order from top to bottom: red, orange, yellow, green, blue, indigo, and violet. The one exception is a double rainbow.

Create an Outdoor Rainbow

Use store-bought bubbles or make your own by mixing water and glycerin. As you blow bubbles, watch for the rainbows to appear on the sides of your bubbles as the light separates.

Science

Insect Chart

To better acquaint your students with insects, create a chart by dividing a large sheet of paper into two parts labeled "INSECTS" and "NOT INSECTS." Cut out many pictures of insects and other creatures that might be mistaken for insects (such as spiders and worms). Have the students sort the pictures and glue them under the appropriate headings on the chart. Hold up one picture at a time. Give students a chance to decide where the creature belongs on the chart. Ask them to explain the reasons for each decision.

Animal/Food Collage

Supply students with pictures of animals and food items found in nature. Instruct each to make a collage to show an animal with the food it would eat. When the activity is completed, students may share their work, telling a little about the eating habits of the animals in their collages.

Critter in Camouflage

When faced with a dangerous situation, insects will often try to escape or hide. Some insects, such as walking sticks and some types of caterpillars, can remain hidden from an enemy because they blend into their surroundings.

Draw and cut out 10 to 12 insects of the same size from brightly colored construction paper. Also cut the same insects from newspaper. Then shred some newspaper into short, thin strips and place these in a medium-sized box. Place all the paper insects in the box and add more shredded newspaper until the box is about half full. Shake the box to mix the contents. Have students take turns digging in the box for colored insects for a set amount of time, such as 30 seconds. Then see how many newsprint insects each student can find in the same amount of time. The conclusion the children will come to is that the camouflaged newsprint insects are much harder to find.

Make-a-Bug!

Provide paper, pencils, and a pair of number cubes. Let students take turns rolling the number cubes to determine what they should draw. A 6 allows them to draw the bug's body; 5, the head; 4, one of the six legs; 3, one of the two antennae; 2, one of the two wings; and 1, one of the two eyes. The antennae and eyes cannot be drawn until the head is in place. The first player to complete a bug is the winner.

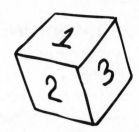

6 = ⭕ body

5 = ⭕ head

4 = ⌒ leg

3 = ⁄ antennae

2 = 🍃 wing

1 = 👁 eye

Spiffy Spider Project

This simple spider project will help reinforce the arachnid anatomy and create a cute display as well. (You will need one for each student.)

Materials:

- 6" (15.2 cm) paper bowl
- 2 to 8 wiggle eyes
- eight 1" x 6" (2.5 cm x 15.2 cm) construction paper strips
- half of a 3" (7.6 cm) construction paper circle
- glue

Directions:

1. Instruct each student to place his bowl upside down and glue the half-circle (head) and eight paper strips (legs) under the rim of the bowl.

2. Have children glue wiggle eyes to the head section. Use the completed project to reinforce that a spider has two main body parts: the combined head and thorax, and the abdomen. The body parts are separated by a narrow waist.

3. Then put these spiffy spiders on double duty to create a unique bulletin-board display. To prepare, cover a bulletin board with black background paper. Staple white yarn in a web design on the paper. Attach the spider projects to the web and add the title, "Who Spies a Spider?"

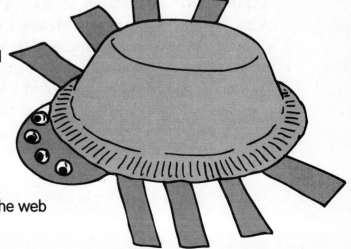

Science

Weather Watching

Introduce the term *meteorologist* to students. Discuss with students what a meteorologist does; then show them. Videotape the weather report on the morning or evening TV news every day. Play it for your class the next day. Discuss the meteorologist's weather predictions. Keep track of how often she is correct. Talk about the difficulties of accurately predicting the weather even with the sophisticated equipment available today.

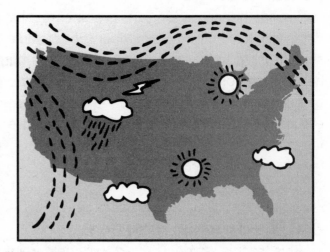

Baby Animals and Their Parents

On one set of index cards, glue pictures of baby animals. On another set, glue pictures of the babies' parents. Have students match each baby animal to its parent. Discuss the names of the baby and parent animals (duck—duckling, sheep—lamb, horse—colt, cow—calf, chicken—chick, goose—gosling, cat—kitten, and dog—puppy).

Bread and Jam For Frances

Read *Bread and Jam For Frances* by Russell Hoban (HarperTrophy, 1993) to your children to get them interested in nutrition. After reading the story of the young badger with the very limited diet, provide pairs of students with large, blank food pyramids. Have students use the book and other materials to put foods in appropriate sections of the chart. Provide a large, labeled chart for references. Have the children illustrate the foods rather than writing names in appropriate sections.

Natural Resources and Products

Make a survey of your community to find out about its natural resources and products. List them in two columns on the chalkboard. Have children tear out pictures from old magazines to illustrate these things. Talk about the importance of natural resources as students glue their pictures on a sheet of poster board and talk about products as they glue those pictures to another sheet of poster board. If possible, bring some samples of these resources and products for students to see, touch, and taste.

Pupil Power

The pupil is the circular opening of the part of the eye called the iris. Muscles at the edge of the pupil can make the opening larger or smaller depending on the amount of light available. When there is a lot of light available, the pupil becomes smaller to allow less of the light in. When there is less light available, the pupil becomes enlarged to allow in as much light as possible. Bring this concept to life for your students with this eye-opening activity.

Darken the room by closing all shades or otherwise blocking windows from light. Have each student choose a partner. Tell the partners to look directly at each other's pupils as you turn out the lights. While everyone's eyes adjust to the darkness, have the partners take note of how large each other's pupils become. Then switch the lights back on. Your students will be amazed at how quickly their partner's pupils "shrink."

After doing this activity a few more times, hand out drawing paper and crayons or markers to students. Have them draw a picture of a time when their pupils would be large (such as bedtime). Then have them turn their papers over and draw a picture to show when their pupils would be small (such as outside on a sunny day). Have older students write a caption for each picture, explaining the reason for the pupil's size. Encourage students to take their pictures home and share their knowledge of "pupil power" with their families.

Tornado in a Bottle

Clean a plastic soda bottle (20 ounce, 1 liter, or 2 liter) inside and out. Fill it with water up to the line where the top of the bottle begins to curve into the neck. Add enough mineral oil so that there's about a half-inch layer on top of the water. Securely tighten the cap. For extra safety, tape it closed.

Holding on to the bottom of the bottle with one hand, quickly rotate the top of the bottle clockwise with the other hand and watch the tornado.

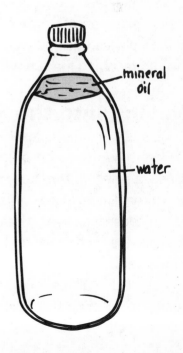

mineral oil

water

Science

Floating Eggs

Materials:

- 2 glasses half-filled with water
- 10 tablespoons (150 ml) of salt
- spoon
- 2 eggs

Directions:

1. Place an egg in one of the half-filled glasses of water.
2. Observe what happens to the egg. (It will sink.)
3. Add the 10 tablespoons (150 ml) of salt to the second half-filled glass of water. Stir well to thoroughly mix the water and salt.
4. Gently place the second egg in the salt water.
5. Observe what happens to the egg. (It will float.)
6. Explain to students that the salt makes the water dense. The denser the water, the greater its buoyancy or its ability to float objects.

Sun, Sun, Mr. Helpful Sun

Is it true that the sun helps water evaporate? Try this experiment to help your students find out. Fill two identical cups to the same level with water. Place one cup in direct sunlight. Place the other cup in a dark cabinet or closet. Check the cups each day and have students mark their findings on a chart. At the end of the experiment, lead students to the conclusion that the sun did help the water evaporate. Extend this experiment by keeping the cups in their places until the water completely evaporates. Of course, the cup receiving the sun will empty first.

Nosing into the Sense of Taste

To taste or not to taste—that is the question. Help children explore how the sense of taste is stronger when helped by the sense of smell. You will need three small paper cups for each child and three different kinds of juice. Have children work with partners as they close their eyes, pinch their noses so they can't smell, drink the juice they are given, and try to guess what it is. Have children try this with all three flavors of juice. Then have them make another taste test of all three flavors with their eyes still closed but their noses not pinched shut. The second time should be much easier with the help of their noses.

The Heart of the Matter

Do these activities in your classroom to give students a better idea of how the heart works and how important it is to take good care of it.

Pumping Action

When blood moves through the heart, it passes from the right side to the left. The left side of the heart is more powerful, as it must pump the blood throughout the entire body. As the blood moves through the heart, it passes through valves that open to allow the blood to pass through, then close so the blood cannot back up. The sound of our heartbeat comes from the opening and closing of these valves as the heart pumps. In order to pump the blood, the heart muscle tightens, then releases. Invite students to simulate this tighten-relax squeezing action by experimenting with an eyedropper or turkey baster and water. Use red food color to tint the water to resemble blood if you wish. Have them note what happens as they tighten, then relax pressure on the bulb. You can also demonstrate this action using an elongated balloon, partially inflated, then tied. Lay the balloon across the palms of both hands, then squeeze the balloon with one hand at a time and observe how the air moves from side to side as you tighten, then release.

Rhythm

Make use of a stethoscope to allow students to listen to the rhythm of their own hearts. Have them to emulate this rhythm with verbal sounds or clapping. Have them jump in place for a few seconds, then use the stethoscope again to hear the rhythm. How has it changed? How does it sound now? Discuss how our hearts beat faster when we exercise because they have to pump more energy (oxygen and food) throughout our systems to maintain peak functioning.

Circulation

It takes about a minute for a gallon of blood to circulate through the body. Pour water with red food coloring into a clean gallon milk jug. Then pour it into a container, timing it to take one minute for the task. Let the children play with the colored water using tubes, funnels, basters, and syringes.

Heart Smart

Name _____

Circle the things that are good for your heart.

Memory and the Brain

Discuss with students how their brains store memories. Play the following memory games to let them test their brains' memory powers.

1. Lay an assortment of ten objects on a tray. Cover the tray with a cloth. Uncover the tray and let a student look at it for about 30 seconds. Cover the tray again and ask the student to name as many objects on the tray as he can remember. Let every child have a turn.

2. Let a child look at the tray of objects for about 30 seconds. Then have the child turn around while you remove one of the objects from the tray. See if the student can identify the missing object. A simpler version of this game is to have students stand in a circle and close their eyes. You quietly remove one child from the circle and ask another child to guess who's missing. Then have that child tell what the missing child was wearing.

Bones and Muscles

Give each student a rubber band to stretch gently. Explain that their muscles work and stretch as easily as the rubber band. Then have students pull their rubber bands as far as they can. Talk about how we sometimes try to stretch our muscles too far. It's best not to stretch muscles too far without proper conditioning. Have students do toe touches and leg stretches. Ask them if they can feel the pull of their muscles.

Have children feel over their bodies to find a large bone (such as a leg), a small bone (such as a finger or toe), and a medium-sized bone (such as the wrist or ankle). Have them describe how their bones feel (hard, straight, and so on). Have students feel the bones in their faces and compare or contrast them to the bones in their bodies.

Lungs

Have students take a deep breath and hold it; then breathe out. Ask them if the air they breathed in was the same air that they breathed out. Explain how their bodies kept the air they breathed in and used it to make their body parts function. Explain that the air they let out was carbon dioxide.

Illustrate how the lungs work by attaching drinking straws to balloons with tape. Have children blow into the straws to expand the balloons.

Science

Liver and Intestines

Hold up a 20-foot (6.1 m) long piece of string. Give it to students and have them line up around the room to stretch the string out to its full length. Explain that this is the length of the small intestine. Cut several 5-foot (1.5 m) long strings. Explain that the large intestine is 5 feet (1.5 m) long. Have students problem solve with the strings to find out how many large intestines it would take to equal the length of the small intestine.

The Stomach

Put soft or crumbly food such as bread, bananas, crackers, and peanut butter in a small, plastic zip-close bag. Add a teaspoon of water and seal the bag tightly. Pass the bag around and let children mash the food in the bag. Then open the bag and take out a spoonful of the mixture. Ask children if they can identify any of the food. Discuss how the stomach breaks down foods and passes them into the body for nutrients.

Shake, Shake, Shake

Here's an activity to "shake up" some enthusiasm for the sense of hearing. Place a variety of small items in film canisters (pennies, uncooked rice, sand, salt, marbles, nails, and so on). Label each lid with a number, beginning with number 1. Make a matching set of canisters and label each with a letter of the alphabet, beginning with **a**.

Let children take turns shaking the canisters, listening to the sound they make. Try to match them by sound. Provide a key for them to check their answers.

For an extra challenge, provide a list of the canisters' contents and have students try to match the canisters to the objects they contain.

Sunlight Is Made of Many Colors

This demonstration helps children see that even though sunlight looks white, it is made up of many colors. On a very sunny day, ask the students what color sunlight is. Most children will say white. Tell the children that you are going to show them a surprise about sunlight.

Spray a fine mist of water out of a garden hose and let the children see for themselves that white light is really made up of many colors. Explain to the students that the water droplets from the hose act like prisms, just like raindrops do in a rainstorm. (A prism is an object such as a soap bubble or even a clear glass of water that can break up white light into colors.) As the sun's light shines through the water droplets, the white light is broken up into red, orange, yellow, green, blue, indigo, and violet—the colors of a rainbow.

Demonstrate this again in the classroom by placing a small mirror into a glass of water (a prism). Position the glass of water so the sun will shine on the mirror. Turn the glass until a rainbow is reflected on a wall.

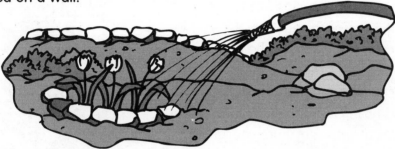

Rainbow Experiment

Materials:

- one pan of water
- a sunny window
- a small mirror
- prisms (if available)

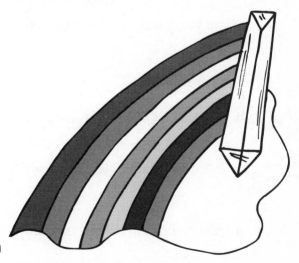

Explain to your students that white light is made up of many colors, and that a rainbow forms when sunlight shines on falling raindrops. As sunlight passes through each drop, it is split up into colors.

Students can make a rainbow indoors on a sunny day. First, have them find a sunny spot in the room. Then have them hold a mirror at an angle in a pan of water with the sun shining on the mirror. A rainbow will appear on the ceiling or wall if the mirror is held still in the water.

If available, let children look at the rainbows that are formed when sunlight shines through prisms.

Science

Bark Rubbings

Show your class pictures of different trees. If your school has trees, take your class out to examine bark. Tell the class that just as people have different fingerprints, trees have different bark patterns. Then have the class make bark rubbings. Have them hold a sheet of drawing paper over a tree trunk. Then color back and forth over the paper with a crayon until there is a print. Repeat the activity with different trees. If possible, label each one with the tree's name. Later, display and compare the rubbings.

A Tree's Age

Show your class a picture of a tree stump or log. Point to the rings and tell the class that one ring (layer) is added to the tree each year. Explain that the tree's age is determined by counting the number of rings. Then tell the children that another method can be used to determine a tree's age. Choose a tree in the schoolyard and have children measure the tree around its trunk about four feet from the ground. Each inch equals about one year in the tree's life. Let students find various ages of nearby trees.

Keeping Toasty Warm

Did you ever wonder how penguins survive the extremely cold temperatures of the South Pole? Here are some interesting facts about how penguins keep warm. Share them with your students.

- Penguins have thick feathers that overlap and keep water and wind away from their bodies.
- Penguins have a thick layer of fat called "blubber" under their skin to insulate them from the cold.
- Penguins may shiver to create additional heat.
- Penguins may stand close together to conserve body heat.

Help your students understand the concept of body heat. Ask them to stand very close together in a large group. After a few minutes ask them if they feel warmer or colder than before. Explain that their combined body heat made the surrounding air temperature rise.

How Walls Protect Us

This simple demonstration will simulate how thick walls help protect people from heat. You will need a chocolate bar, broken in half. Place one half of the chocolate bar on a plate in the sun on a hot day. Place the other half in a simple shelter made of several bricks. Make sure the shelter does not allow any sunlight in. Using a stopwatch, time how long it takes for the exposed chocolate bar to melt. When it has melted, remove the bricks from the shelter and observe the chocolate that was protected from the sun. Then discuss with your students the fact that in hot, dry climates, people often build homes with thick walls.

Wonderful Waves

Waves are caused by wind—the stronger the wind, the bigger the waves.

Provide several 9" x 13" (22.8 cm x 33cm) or larger metal or plastic pans filled with water to about two inches from the top. Place them on towels, or do this activity outside. Let the children try blowing gently, and then more forcefully, to make waves. Ask them which waves are bigger.

Fill a clear plastic soda or water bottle halfway with water tinted with blue food coloring. Fill the rest of the bottle to the top with vegetable oil. Cap it securely. Show the children how to hold the bottle on its side and gently shake it to create an ocean full of foaming waves.

A Sea Safari

For this classification activity featuring animals of the ocean, you will need picture cards of many different ocean animals. Also have students decorate your room by creating ocean murals to fill the walls. For an underwater atmosphere, hang blue streamers from the ceiling. Hide the ocean animal cards around the room. Have students work in groups to find a designated number of animal cards as they wander around the room (quietly, so they don't frighten the animals). After finding all their cards, the members of each group should work together to classify the ocean animals into categories such as marine mammals, fish, birds, reptiles, etc. Have each group create a graph to record their findings. When all groups have completed their graphs, have them compare their findings.

© McGraw-Hill Children's Publishing

0-7682-2526-4 *Fast Ideas for Busy Teachers*

Social Studies

"Cornered" Game

Label the north wall of your classroom. Have students label the other walls south, east, and west accordingly. Choose a student to be "it." Blindfold that child. Tell the rest of the students to choose and stand under one of the cardinal direction labels around the room. The student who is "it" must choose one of the directions. If "north" is chosen, all the students standing under the "north" label have to sit down. The remaining students may choose a new place to stand (north, south, east or west). "It" chooses another direction and the students standing in that area sit down. Continue the game until only one student is left standing. That person is "it" for the next game. Students not only have a good time playing this game, they learn their directions at the same time.

Directional Desks

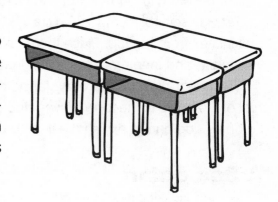

Arrange your students' desks into groups of four to form tables. When students line up or pass papers, have them do it according to compass directions. For example, say, "Pass your papers to the person in the northwest corner of your group" or, "The west side of each group may line up." This procedure really helps students learn directions and is a unique way of assigning tasks.

What's in a Name?

The names of streets or roads in a community often date back several generations. If you live in an older community, ask senior citizens or your local librarian to help you discover why your streets have certain names. Make a list to share with the class. You may also want to find out how your city or town was named. Let students guess, then tell them the facts.

Postcards

Here's a creative way to integrate social studies with letter-writing skills. Have your students make their own postcards after completing a social studies unit about a city, state, country, or continent. Give each student an unruled 4" x 7" (10.1 cm x 17.7 cm) index card. Have the students draw a picture of a favorite area on one side of the card. Then have the students draw a line down the middle of the other side. Direct the students to write you a message on the left half. Have the students design a stamp on the right half and address the card to you at school. Then have the children "mail" the postcard. (Use a paper-covered box with a slit cut in the top as a mailbox.) Share the cards with the class by passing them around or displaying them on a bulletin board.

Homes for Everyone

Teach your students these concepts about homes:

- Homes are needed to protect people from the weather and from other dangers, such as wild animals.
- Climate, materials available, and possible dangers are the main factors that determine the kinds of homes people build.

Discuss with the children the kinds of homes found in your school's community. Review the climate of the area and ask how the homes are adapted to the climate. (For example, ask, "Are there slanted roofs for snow and rainfall? Air conditioners to combat heat? Storm windows for wintertime? Trees to provide shade?") When your students have an understanding of why homes are different from place to place, have them independently complete the activity "My Mini-Book About Houses" (page 94). Or you may wish to use the page as a directed teaching activity. Read each description to your students and have them suggest types of homes that one might see in each area. Then let the children draw the homes on the page.

Home Sweet Sack

Show a sketch or photo of your home to the students and tell them it is a picture of a place that is special to you. Ask the class to guess the place. After it has been identified as your home, ask why homes are important. (Examples: People can relax at home; a home protects us from the cold.) Tell the class that every person needs a place to live and to be protected from rain, wind, and other forces of nature. Explain that a home (or shelter) is a basic need for all people.

Then give each child a paper lunch sack, a few sheets of newspaper, a six-inch (15.2 cm) paper square, and scraps of colored paper to make a model of a home. Have the students follow these directions:

1. Cut out paper features such as doors, windows, and shutters, and glue them to the bag.
2. Fold the square in half to make a roof. Draw shingles on the roof or glue on a chimney.
3. Stuff the bag with crumpled newspaper, fold the top over, and staple the roof to the top of the bag.
4. Design a special mailbox, cut it out, and glue it to the side or front of your home.

After the students are finished, display the homes along a shelf or table.

My Mini-Book About Houses

Name _____

My Mini-Book About
Houses

Some houses are in hot, wet places that have a lot of plants.

Some houses are in hot, dry places that have no trees.

Some houses are in cold places that get snow and have trees.

Some houses are in cold, snowy places that do not have trees.

Here is a picture of my house.

Who's Who

Use waiting time to teach and quiz your students about people in the community and the news. For example, you might ask, *Who's the President of the United States?* Occasionally, write names on the chalkboard so that your students learn to recognize the President's name as well as other important names. Challenge your students to master the current "Who's Who" list. Your students will be eager participants.

People at Work

Let your students make a colorful collage showcasing the variety of jobs people have. Have the students cut out magazine pictures of people at work and glue them onto a sheet of butcher paper. Have the students include labels with their pictures. Display the collage during your students' study of careers as a reminder of the many career choices that are available.

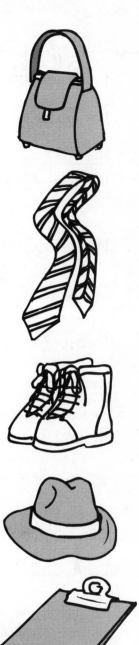

Dress for the Job

Set up a dress-up corner in your classroom where children can role-play different jobs. Parents may be able to donate old clothing and accessories for your corner. Let the students explore the corner in their free time. As they dress up in costumes or play with particular objects, ask them to tell you about the workers they are portraying. Join in the fun by pretending to be a patient, a customer, or any other person that fits in with the role-playing at the time.

Interviewing Parents at Home

Here's a great way for children to learn about jobs and appreciate the work their parents do. As a homework assignment, have each student ask a parent for an interview. Instruct the students to prepare their questions ahead of time by writing them down. Questions should include the following: "What kinds of duties do you have?" "What helped you decide to get into your line of work?" "What qualities should a person have to do your job?" Then have the students conduct the interviews. Later, have the children give oral reports on their parents' jobs.

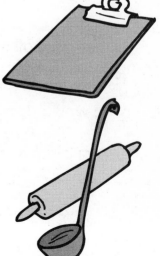

A Special Community Helper

Person being interviewed: _____

Date: _____

What is your job title? _____

_____

Where do you work? (Examples: in an office, at a park) _____

_____

_____

Please describe your work in two or three sentences. _____

_____

_____

Do you work with special equipment? If yes, please explain. _____

_____

_____

What do you think is the most interesting thing about your job? _____

_____

_____

Is there any other information about your work you'd like to share?

(Examples: the kind of training or schooling required, the type of person

who would do well in your line of work) _____

_____

_____

_____

_____

Life-Size Community Helpers

Have students make community helpers from outlines of themselves. First, have each student lie on a sheet of butcher paper while you draw around her. Then have students cut out their outlines. Next, have each child draw features and glue paper clothing onto her outline to show what kind of community helper she'd like to be when she grows up. Later, display the figures on a wall or in the hallway.

Handpicked Community Helpers

Challenge your class with this decision-making activity. Have students pretend they are in charge of forming a new community that will be gradually populated. Then divide your class into small cooperative groups, and instruct students in each group to list five community helpers they'd want in the community from the start. Afterwards, let the groups share their lists with the class and explain how they decided on their choices.

Career Brainstorm

Here's a fun way to begin to teach young children about careers. Have each child trace his hand on a piece of white paper. Then have him write a career choice on the palm (many students will write the career their mother or father has) and write on each finger something a person in that career might touch. Lots of great ideas come out of this "brainstorming."

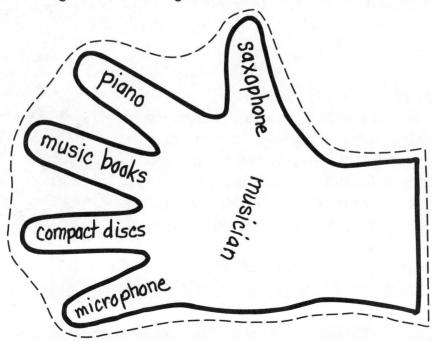

Social Studies

Around the World with Ocean Animals

On a map or globe, show students the different oceans of the world. Divide the class into groups to research and report on marine life in different places. For example, one group might report on a coral reef, another group might report on the Antarctic Ocean, and a third group could report on Atlantic coastal waters. A list of simple questions such as these can guide students:

1. What ocean animals are common in your area?
2. Are there any ocean animals that live only in your area and never leave it?
3. Are there any endangered ocean animals in your area?
4. What is the weather like in your area?

Encourage students to look in library books and reference books. Geography books about different areas of the world will be helpful. When reports have been completed, let groups share what they have learned with their classmates.

We All Share the Same Needs

Tell the class that people all around the world share the same basic needs. Explain that physical needs include being fed and being protected from the elements. Add that people also have emotional needs such as being loved, feeling safe, and having a sense of belonging.

Then let the children look at books and brochures to learn about families in different countries. Later, have each child use what he or she found out to design a poster titled "We All Share the Same Needs."

Thanks, Mom and Dad!

Brainstorm with the students what their parents have to do in order to provide food, clothing, and other basic needs for their families. List the ideas on the chalkboard. (Examples: They go to work to earn money, go grocery shopping, cook the meals, buy or sew clothes, and pay the mortgage or rent.) Then, have the children write thank-you letters to their parents telling how much they appreciate the things their parents do for them.

Sing a Geography Song

Teach this song to help your students remember the names of the continents and oceans. It's sung to the tune of "He's Got the Whole World in His Hands."

"We've Got the Whole World in Our Hands"

We've got the whole world in our hands,
We've got the whole world in our hands,
We've got the whole world in our hands,
We've got the whole world in our hands.

We've got North and South America in our hands,
We've got Europe, Asia, and Africa in our hands,
We've got Australia and Antarctica in our hands,
We've got the continents in our hands.

We've got the Indian Ocean in our hands,
We've got the Arctic Ocean in our hands,
We've got the Atlantic and Pacific oceans in our hands,
We've got the oceans in our hands.

Repeat Verse 1

The song can be expanded to include landforms ("We've got the mountains and the deserts in our hands, We've got the rainforests and the rivers in our hands . . ."), animals, people, countries, etc.

Mystery Parts

Put items associated with famous Americans on a bulletin board. For example: Lincoln's stovepipe hat, George Washington's cherry tree, and Ben Franklin's kite. Ask your class to decide which American belongs to each item and write a sentence or story about each person.

Lincoln's Love of Reading

Abraham Lincoln loved to read books. Challenge students to think of books they have read. If they could have loaned a book to Abe, which book do they think he would have enjoyed reading? Why? What did the student enjoy about the book?

Social Studies

Patriotic Song of the Month

As a part of your morning routine, sing a patriotic song. At the beginning of each month, teach your class a new song such as: "Yankee Doodle," "America," "The Star-Spangled Banner," "This is My Country," "God Bless America," "America the Beautiful," "This Land is Your Land," and "The Battle Hymn of the Republic." By the end of the month, they will be able to sing it perfectly and be ready for the next song. Discuss the meaning of the words and how they are significant to our country. You might also want to talk about who wrote the songs and the circumstances behind them.

America—A Special Country

Talk with the class about the kinds of feelings Americans might have about their country and why. Guide students into seeing how the ideas of freedom and democracy served as the foundation for the country, and how they influenced the way America evolved as a nation.

Give each student a copy of the scroll pattern on page 101. Have them write about what they like about their country and why it is special. Have students sign their names at the bottom of the scroll. Then instruct them to cut out the scroll. Display the papers on a bulletin board. Twist red, white and blue crepe paper streamers, and tape or pin them along the sides of the board for a colorful border.

Snapshots of Famous Women

Choose a famous woman in history. Invite your students to imagine that they were present during an important event in her life. Talk about what event that would be. Have them imagine taking snapshots of the event. Give each child drawing paper and crayons or markers to draw her snapshot. Walk around to each child and have her dictate a photo caption to you to write at the bottom of the drawing. Post the snapshots on a bulletin board. To give the display an old-fashioned photo album look, the children can glue black paper triangles on the corners of the drawings. Add the title "We Were There When . . ." to finish the display.

A Special Country

Name _____

Think about why you like living in the United States. Then write at least three reasons why America is a special place to live.

America's Flag

Use the code to color the flag below. Then cut out the flag and glue it to a cardboard handle. Wave your flag or display it on America's birthday.

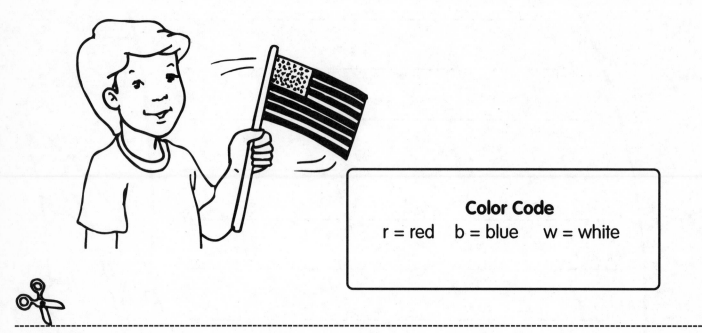

Color Code

r = red   b = blue   w = white

Art

Lion Fans

One of the many products made in China is the fan. If possible, share several examples of hand-held fans with the children and point out any "Made in China" stickers. As the lion is one of several animal symbols for the Chinese New Year, have your children make lion fans. Provide them with small paper plates and have them use brown marker to color around the edge of their plates. Demonstrate how to use scissors to fringe the brown area, creating a mane. Next, use markers or paper scraps and glue to create faces for their lions. Finally, use tape or glue to attach a craft stick or tongue depressor handle to each plate, creating a fan.

Foliage Friends

Let children create their own leafy friends from magazines, markers, scissors, glue, and leaves of various sizes and shapes. Have each child look through magazines to find and cut out a friendly looking face. Ask them to glue the face to a sheet of white paper. Then have children glue large leaves under the faces to represent the leaf person's body. Invite them to add other leaves for arms, legs, and a hat.

Noisemakers

These "Earth Shakers" will get everybody moving. Give each student two small, white paper plates. Using markers, crayons, or paints, have each student decorate the bottom sides of the plates to resemble Earth. Glue strips of blue or green tissue paper to the uncolored side of one plate. Help students staple their plates together almost all the way around. Then add a handful of uncooked rice into each noisemaker, and finish stapling the shakers all the way around. Then let the shaking begin.

Mini Mice Craft

Children will enjoy making this simple, tiny mouse. Turn half an empty walnut shell upside down. Cut two small mouse ears and a long tail from ribbon or fabric. Glue the ears and tail on the shell. Add two small craft wiggly eyes. Glue on a small pom-pom for a nose.

Art

Holiday Placemat

Design holiday placemats to be treasured from year to year.

Materials:

* 12" x 18" (30.4 cm x 45.7 cm) sheets of construction paper
* markers
* pens
* clear self-adhesive plastic (or laminate)

Directions:

1. Have each student write the name of the placemat recipient at the top of a sheet of construction paper. Below the name, have them write a message to that person that tells why the student is happy to have this person in her life.
2. Have the students illustrate their placemats.
3. Cover the placemats with self-adhesive plastic or laminate them.

Celebrate Green!

Put the following materials on a table in your classroom: white and green paper, white and green glue, items such as milk bottle caps, Easter grass, green cotton balls, tissue paper, fabric scraps and ribbons, stickers, glitter, crayons, markers, paints, and so on.

Let students choose the materials they want to create green collages. Mount the collages on a bulletin board under the caption "Let's Celebrate Green!"

Spring Garden Collage

Let each child cut pictures of flowers from magazines and seed or flower catalogs. Next glue them on a sheet of construction paper to form a spring flower garden. Display these collages around the classroom for a "breath of spring air."

Nifty Necklaces

Give each student a large, white paper plate. Have students cut through the ridged rim, then cut out the center of the circle. Ask students to decorate the lower portion of the ring to resemble Earth using crayons, markers, or paints. Then have students use black markers or crayons to write Earth Day phrases around the upper portion of the ring ("Earth—There's No Place Like Home;" "Honor the Earth;" "Keep Earth Beautiful;" and so on). Ask students to wear their necklaces to show their respect for Earth.

Tissue Paper Snow Hills

It's easy to create a mound of snow using white tissue paper. Just gather the tissue paper and form it in the appropriate shape. Tape or staple the paper so it will hold its shape. Then tape or staple the paper to a wall or bulletin board for an easy three-dimensional effect. Then add your students' renditions of their favorite snow toys such a toboggans and snowboards.

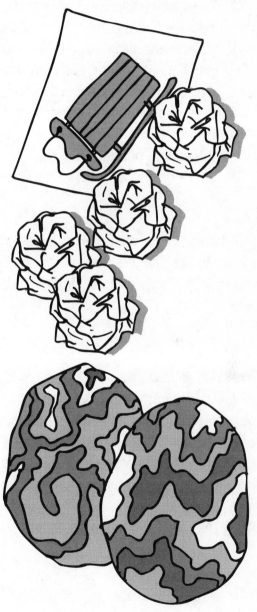

Watercolor Eggs

Cut coffee filters into egg shapes. Provide colored markers so children can draw lines and designs on the egg shapes. Limit the amount of colors they use or the egg colors will run black. Fold the eggs over three or four times, let children quickly dip them in a bowl of water, and then unfold them and place them on paper towels to dry. The colors will run together and make pretty eggs to decorate the classroom walls, bulletin boards, or windows.

Squiggle Art

Draw squiggles of various kinds on blank sheets of paper. Hand out a different squiggle sheet to each student. Encourage students to create anything they can imagine out of their squiggles. Be prepared for some great pictures.

Art

Vegetable Printing

Let students use fresh vegetables to make fun and interesting prints and designs with paint. Pour small amounts of tempera paint or poster paint into foam trays that have sides (to avoid paint slopping over). Then bring out the veggies and let students dip them in the paint.

1. Cut an apple in half in any direction.
2. Cut a fresh potato in half and use the flat side to make prints. Carve designs into the flat side for different effects.
3. Roll an ear of corn in the paint. Use two spoons to pick it up and place it onto paper. Roll it around for a different effect.
4. Cut an ornamental gourd in half.
5. Use whole or sliced string beans to create lines and curves.
6. Lettuce and other greens have fancy-shaped leaves that can make interesting printed patterns.
7. Pears and other fruits with interesting shapes make fun designs.

Tips for Fruit and Vegetable Printing:

When printing with fruits and vegetables, use forks or corn-on-the-cob holders to keep fingers clean. These holders make it easier for small hands to handle the fruits and vegetables and avoid smudging.

Puffing Puffs

A popular form of art in China is origami, the art of paper folding. Books and craft kits on this subject are readily available. Chinese children play a hopping frog game using this art form. After folding their papers into mini frogs, they place them on a table, then blow at them from behind to see which frog will get to the opposite end of the table first. You can try a similar game with your students using cotton balls. Have the children race each other in pairs or have them work independently at getting their cotton "frogs" from one end of a table to the other. The cotton balls can be decorated with green marker or bits of paper, felt, and glue.

© McGraw-Hill Children's Publishing

0-7682-2526-4 *Fast Ideas for Busy Teachers*

Plastic Egghead People with Grass Hair

These adorable egghead people are made by first hot gluing the opposite ends of plastic a egg together. The smaller end of the egg forms the body and the larger end forms the top for the face.

Put a pea-size dab of hot glue on the flatter end of the egg; then place the pointed end of the egg on the glue. Hold it tight so the hot glue melts the plastic a little. It only takes a few seconds. (Prepare eggs without students for safety.)

Let students carefully use paints or permanent markers to make a face on the top and a shirt or dress on the bottom. Add bows and bow ties. Instruct students to plant grass seed in soil in the open top of the egghead.

To speed up germination of the grass seed, put the heads in a small, flat box and slide the box into a clear plastic bag. Tie the bag shut so that it's sealed. In two or three days, the seeds will sprout and grow up to an inch (2.54 cm). The bag acts as a mini green-house and keeps the seeds moist.

As the grass grows, students can give their eggheads custom haircuts.

Hot Glue

Art

Paper Plate Pinecone

Materials:
- 1 paper plate
- 1 brown pipe cleaner (chenille stem)
- ribbon
- brown watercolor
- clear tape

Directions:
1. Cut a pinecone shape from the center of a paper plate.
2. Cut the rim off the plate and cut the rim into strips.
3. Tape the strips to the pinecone shape, layering each strip, and taping it in the center.
4. Trim the edges with scissors.
5. Punch a hole in the top of the pinecone. Push a piece of pipe cleaner through the hole and make a loop hanger.
6. Lightly paint the pinecone with brown watercolor.
7. Tie a ribbon to the hanger/stem.

Glow-in-the-Dark Pictures

Let students create their own glow-in-the-dark pictures using iridescent paint on black or dark blue construction paper. Have children use pencils to sketch simple pictures; then let them go over the lines with crayon or colored chalk. Any lines they want to show up in the dark should be traced in iridescent paint. (These lines might include eyes, fangs, the moon, a ghostly outline, etc.) Display the pictures for everyone to see. Turn out the lights to get the full effect.

Creative Creatures

Bring a variety of old magazines to class. Let students look through them and cut out pictures of different parts of animals, people, and objects. Have them arrange the parts on paper to create wacky new creatures, then glue down the pieces. Mount the creative creatures on a classroom wall or bulletin board for everyone to enjoy.

Seasonal Trees

Have students work in pairs, tracing each other's arm and spread-out hand on large sheets of paper. Challenge them to use their creativity to turn these into trees with the arm as the trunk and the fingers as branches. Provide construction paper and tissue paper in a variety of colors for students to tear and glue on for leaves. Let each student choose whether to make a spring, summer, fall, or winter tree.

Wheelbarrow Planter

Materials:
- laundry detergent scoop
- tacky craft glue
- 2 milk bottle lids
- potting soil
- flower seeds
- stickers and other decorative items

Directions:
1. Glue a milk bottle lid to each side of the scoop near the bottom front corners for wheels.
2. Decorate the scoop with stickers or other decorative items.
3. Fill the scoop about half full of potting soil.
4. Plant flower seeds in the soil.
5. Set the wheelbarrow planter in a sunny place and water it regularly. Transplant the seedlings when they are about three inches tall.

Art

Giant Weather Mobile

Materials:

- 2 paper plates
- paint
- white poster board
- scissors
- string or yarn
- hole punch

Directions:

1. Paint both paper plates yellow. Let them dry; then staple them face-to-face all around.
   Punch one hole at the top and one at the bottom.

2. Cut a 15" (38.1 cm) rainbow shape from poster board. Paint the rainbow and let it dry. Punch a hole at the center of the top and four holes at the bottom.

3. Cut out and paint a cloud, lightning bolt, large raindrop, and snowflake shape. Punch a hole at the top of each shape.

4. Attach a string hanger to the top of the paper plate sun. Use string to connect the bottom of the sun and the rainbow. Then hang the smaller shapes from the bottom of the rainbow.

Jar Lid Magnet

Materials:

- clean metal jar lid
- photo, drawing, or message (to fit inside the lid)
- pencil
- scissors
- glue
- small magnetic strip
- narrow ribbon or trim

Directions:

1. Center the lid over the photo, drawing, or message and trace around it.
2. Cut out the circle and glue it inside the lid.
3. Glue the magnetic strip on the back of the lid.
4. Glue ribbon or trim to the edge of the lid to decorate it.
5. Put the completed magnet on the refrigerator door.

Decorative Art

Materials:
- an object to decorate (clay pot, plastic-foam cup, cardboard frame, and so on)
- decorative material (dried beans, pebbles, buttons, eggshells, etc.)
- tacky craft glue

Directions:
1. Arrange the decorative items on the object you want to decorate until you have the look you want. Then glue them on the object.
2. For a glossy finish, paint over the object with tacky craft glue and let it dry.
3. Use the completed craft for a decoration or give it to someone for a gift.

- Wash eggshells before using them. To give eggshells an ancient look, use water to dilute water-based black paint and rub it on the shells.

Primary Art Ideas
- What does an old-fashioned record player have to do with art? Put a paper plate on the turntable where the record should go. Then turn the machine on and let students use watercolors to paint designs on the plate as it goes around.

- Show students how to use big marshmallows and toothpicks to make snowmen. You'll need three big marshmallows held together by toothpicks. Use food coloring to draw on facial features.

An Apple Tree's Year

Your students will enjoy learning how an apple tree changes throughout the year. To make an apple tree book, provide each student with one 12" x 18" (30.4 cm x 45.7 cm) sheet of blue construction paper. Have them fold the paper in half vertically to make it 9" x 12" (22.8 cm x 30.4 cm). Then ask them to unfold the paper and draw a tree trunk that starts at the bottom of the paper and goes to the fold. Above the fold, have them extend the trunk and add bare branches. Have students create tiny snowflakes from white paper. Glue the tiny snowflakes around the bare tree branches. Then label the top of the paper "Winter."

On the next day, give each student a 9" x 12" (22.8 cm x 30.4 cm) sheet of blue construction paper. Have them align the paper so it covers the top half of the winter picture. Then ask students to redraw the bare branches of the apple tree. Have them make a spring scene by using green paint to make fingerprint leaves. Then have them create pink and white blossoms from crumpled tissue paper pieces and glue them to the tree when the paint is dry. Label the top of the paper "Spring." Staple the finished page to the top of the winter scene along the left side.

Continue in the same way, making summer and fall pages. For summer, have students use green paint to make fingerprint leaves. For fall, have students use red, yellow, or green paint to make fingerprint apples. Have each student choose a favorite color of apple to feature on the tree. Be sure to label the summer and fall trees. This will create a four-page booklet. When all four pages are done, have students add the title "An Apple Tree's Year" at the bottom of the tree trunk.

Physical Education

Bunny Bowling

You will need ten clean 2-liter soda bottles with a small amount of water in each for stability. Decorate the bottles by gluing or taping tag board bunny cutouts on them. Place the bottles in a 4-3-2-1 triangle. Have a child roll a soft ball and try to knock down the bottles. Have the children count the bottles as they are set up and count the ones that are knocked over. Use this game for other holidays by changing the tag board cutouts to match the holiday or season.

Smiley Sheet Toss

Create your own parachute from an old or frayed bed sheet. Spread a large-as-possible, light-colored sheet on a workspace. Use a dark marker to draw a dinner plate-sized smiley face in the center. About 12" (30.4 cm) from each side of the face, draw saucer-sized smiley faces aligned diagonally with the sheet's corner. Put the folded sheet in a carry-all bag with six beanbags.

Spread the sheet on the floor or ground and let each child claim a spot along its edges. Have the children bend down, grip the edge closest to them, and lift the sheet. Practice ripple movements as a group; then toss a beanbag onto the sheet. Challenge the children to make the beanbag land on the large smiley face. Then add a second beanbag. Explain that the center smiley face must remain "beaned" as players manipulate the sheet to move the second beanbag onto one of the smaller faces. When that's done, continue by moving a third beanbag onto the final smiley face without moving the others. Finally, throw all the beanbags onto the sheet. See how long the children can keep the beanbags jumping like corn popping in a popper. An escaped bag ends the game.

Scoop the Ball

Cut off the bottom of a clean, plastic bottle ($1/2$ to 1 gallon) with a handle. Trim the remainder of the bottles into a scoop shape. Cover the scoop edge with freezer tape or colorful plastic tape. Attach a strong cord to a rubber or plastic ball. Attach the other end of the cord to the handle of the bottle.

Hold the bottle by the handle with the open end up, swing the ball outward and up, and catch it in the bottle.

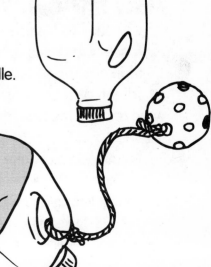

← Cut.

Physical Education

Playground Exploration

Equipment: any existing playground equipment; cones, hoops, trees, and other kinds of obstacles

Procedure: Set up a course around the playground that leads the children around trees, over cones, through a sandbox, over monkey bars, and wherever else on the playground you want the students to run. Lead the way or draw a simple diagram and show the students the course ahead of time. Tell the students to begin at the starting point and continue around the playground until they have completed the course. Help the students keep track of their time with stopwatches if you have them. If you have the students repeat this activity, encourage them to better their time.

How Far Can You Jump?

Introduce your students to two field events. Be sure to warm them up first with stretching exercises. You'll need a sand pit or a large mat for these jumps.

Standing Broad Jump: A student stands behind a line marked near the edge of the sand pit or mat. With his arms back and down, the student jumps forward, swinging his arms forward and up. Measure the distance from the line to the part of the body that lands closest to the line.

Running Long Jump: Make a chalk line near the edge of the sand pit or mat and a second line about 20 feet behind the first line. A student stands behind the second line. She runs to the first line and jumps onto the sand or mat, landing on two feet. Measure the distance from the first line to the part of the body that lands closest to it.

Record the distances and let the children try to improve them on another day.

Touch and Go

Equipment: any playground equipment and permanent playground structures (poles, backstop, trees)

Procedure: Tell the students that they will be given two minutes to run and touch as many playground objects as possible. (For older students, provide a list on chart paper.) They can touch the objects in any order they prefer. After the activity, ask how many students touched five objects, eight objects, and so on. Repeat the activity if possible.

Exercise, Fun, and Games

Golf Tee Jumping Contest: Strengthen your students' physical skills as they practice measuring length. Give each student a golf tee and a strip of masking tape. Have each student write her name on the tape and place the tape around the tee. Identify a starting line in a grassy area and mark it with two tees. (If you don't have a grassy area, do this activity on the blacktop and mark with chalk.) Have the students one at a time stand on the starting line and do a broad jump. Tell the student to place her tee in the grass at the landing spot. (To save time, mark three starting lines so several students can jump simultaneously.) After all the students have jumped, let them use yardsticks to measure from the starting line to their tees. You can also have the students cut yarn the length of their jumps and measure the yarn later. The students can mount the yarn lengths horizontally on a bulletin board to graph their jumps.

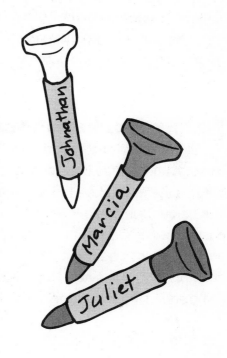

Beanball: Give each student a large dried bean and have him decorate it or write his initials on it. Set five large, plastic bowls on the floor about two feet (.61 m) apart. Have five or six students stand about ten steps away from each bowl and try to toss their beans into the bowl. After the students toss their beans, let them use a centimeter ruler to measure the distance from the bowl to their beans. (Younger students can measure with cubes or craft sticks.) The student whose bean was closest to the bowl earns one point. If a student's bean lands in the bowl, he or she earns two points. The students can toss their beans again and accumulate points until you end the game.

Physical Education

Four Corner Challenge

Equipment: four cones, four tag board or construction paper signs, tape

Use the cones to designate a 35-foot-square (10.6 m) play area. Write a different locomotive movement such as jump and skip, crawl and crab walk, and gallop and hop on each side of every sign. Tape a sign on each cone. (You might draw an arrow on each sign to indicate the direction of movement from cone to cone.)

Divide the class into four groups and have each group start at a different sign. If you do this activity inside, you can play music to signal the students to begin. When the music stops, the students stop and change directions. When the music starts again, the children begin to move. (If played outside, use a whistle or a command as a signal.) When the children change direction, they perform the movement on the back of the sign. You can also incorporate different types of equipment. The children can toss beanbags, bounce balls, or tap balloons while they move.

Wacky Hockey Practice

All you need are four new toilet brushes (the bristle type), two jar lids, a chair, and a smooth, uncarpeted floor for a wild introduction to hockey. Set the chair at one end of the play area as the goal. Have the children line up at the opposite end of the play area. Give the first four students in line a toilet-brush hockey stick each. The first two students use their sticks to pass a jar-lid hockey puck back and forth toward the goal and then try to make a goal. The puck must pass between the two front chair legs for a goal to be scored. Once the first pair attempts a goal, the next two children in line start passing the second puck. The first pair goes to the end of the line, giving the sticks and puck to those at the front of the line. The activity continues until each child has had a predetermined number of turns.

Slow Down, Jack!

Some young children have a hard time with coordination, and jumping jacks are often difficult for them. During your warm-up time, say very slowly, "I would like to see ten super slow jumping jacks." They will think this is fun, and will do their jumping jacks very slowly. This slow practice helps them learn each step in the exercise. As you continue doing the exercise, direct them to go faster and faster until they are going super fast.

How Do They Move?

Have the children stand in light plastic hoops. Let them warm up by doing jumping and stretching exercises inside their hoops. Then have each child move from his or her hoop to a nearby hoop while imitating different animal locomotion. Ask, for example, How does an elephant move? How does a snake move? How does a horse move? How does a kangaroo move? Remind the students to move without running into other students and to wait in each hoop until you give them the next question.

Line-Up Madness

This is a fun game for listening skills and lining up. For the last five minutes of gym or recess, play "Freeze." When you say, Go! the children can run around like crazy. When they hear you blow your whistle, they must "freeze" in whatever position they happen to be. If someone wiggles or moves just a little bit and you see them, they are sent to line up and get ready to go back to class. Eventually everyone should be in line.

Step-by-Step Relay

Each relay team needs two sheets of paper (cardboard, plastic, or fabric works also). Divide a straight course into as many sections as there are members on a team, and have each team member stand at the beginning of her section. At the starting signal, the first team member lays down one sheet of paper and steps onto it. Next, she lays down the second sheet and steps onto it. Then she picks up the first sheet, lays it down in front, and steps onto it. The first team member continues, stepping only on the paper, until she reaches the next team member, who continues in the same fashion. The first team to reach the end of the course wins. One variation is to use longer sheets of paper and have each four-person team move along the course as a unit.

Physical Education

Indoor Snowballs

All you need for this active game are three small soft foam balls. These are the "snowballs." Have your students make a circle. Choose three throwers, give them each a snowball, and have them stand in the middle of the circle. The throwers will try to hit the other players with the snowballs. They must throw below the shoulders. When you say "One!" the other players may walk away from the throwers; when you say "Two!" the players may run away; when you say "Three!" the throwers may run after the other players. If a player is hit by a snowball, he must sit cross-legged on the floor. If he catches the snowball, he becomes the new thrower. If the player tries to catch the snowball and misses, he must sit cross-legged on the floor. The player can get back in the game by tagging another player (not a thrower), but this must be done while sitting cross-legged and without moving from the original spot. When all the players are down, and only the throwers are left, the throwers choose new throwers and the game starts again.

For a faster game, use six snowballs and choose six throwers.

Line Moves

Put the children in groups of eight. Have each group stand and hold hands to form a line. Let the lines experiment with some of these moves:

- Make a circle, a square, a triangle, an oval, a diamond, etc.
- Make these letters: B, C, D, G, J, L, M, N, O, P, R, S, U, V, W, Z.
- Walk together in a pattern, such as left, forward, forward (one step to the left, two steps forward) or right, forward, forward, left (one step right, two steps forward, one step left).
- Pretend you are a piece of string. Stretch yourself out and then wind yourself up. Tie yourself in a knot.

Parachute Fitness

Equipment: parachute, music (optional)

Here are some warm-ups that incorporate a variety of fitness activities. Have the children stand evenly around the parachute and follow these directions:

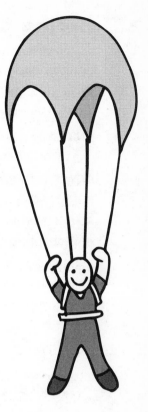

- Jogging—stand sideways to the parachute and hold onto it with your right hand. Jog while moving clockwise; then change directions.
- Jumping Jacks—stand sideways to the parachute and hold onto it with your right hand. Stretch out your arms so the parachute is tight. Perform a set of jumping jacks; then change hands and do another set.
- Leg Lifts—lie down with the parachute over your legs. Hold the parachute taut just under your chin. Keeping your legs straight, lift them one at a time, and then both together, raising the parachute off the floor.
- Sit-ups—sit on the floor with your legs under the parachute. Hold the parachute so it is taut. Bend your knees and lie down on your back. Now come up to a sitting position, holding on to the parachute.
- Toe Touches—hold the parachute with both hands so it is taut. Lift the parachute above your head and then down to the floor as you touch your toes.

Over-and-Under Relay

Equipment: one playground ball per team

Procedure: Place the students in equal teams. Have each team stand in a relay line. Give the first person in each team a playground ball. The object is for each team to get a ball from the front of the line to the back without dropping it. The first person in each line hands the ball over her head to the next person. That person then hands the ball under his legs to the next person. This pattern continues until the ball reaches the last person in the line. The relay can either stop there or the same pattern can continue back to the first person.

Physical Education

Spring Sprouts

For this rousing spring version of "Simon Says," choose two flowers that have seeds, such as poppies and petunias. Prepare a set of simple paper flowers for each flower team. Then give each child a flower and tell the children the flower names.

Call "Scatter the seeds!" The children spread out and crouch down in the play area, hiding their flowers. Then call "Sprout, sprout, little _____," and fill in the blank with one of the two flower names or simply flowers. Students holding the flower called spring up quickly and hold up their flowers. All the children spring up when you call "Sprout, sprout, little flowers." If a child fails to jump up quickly when her flower is called, or if a child jumps up when the other flower is called, her team scores a point. The team with the fewest points at the end of the period wins.

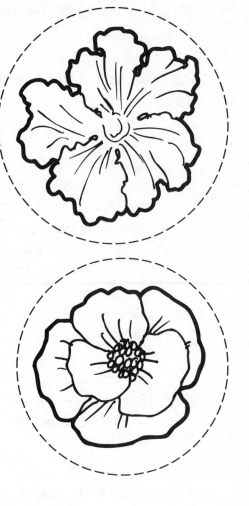

Variations:

- With older children, form three or four flower teams and pick up the pace.
- Call out additional stages of life, such as "Bloom, bloom, little poppy" and "Wither, wither, little petunia." Have the children respond accordingly.
- Let a student be the caller.

Cone Relay

Equipment: four or five cones per relay team, playground balls, soccer balls, basketballs, large plastic hoops, and jump ropes

Procedure: Have the students form relay teams. Place four or five cones in a line in front of each team for the students to travel around. Have the first student in each line obtain a type of equipment that you designate. The first person must travel around all five cones and back with his equipment in the manner that you determine. Here are some movements for your students to try:

- Ball—dribble it, bounce it, or toss and catch it
- Hoop—roll it, swing it on your arm, or swing it around your waist
- Jump rope—skip with it around one cone and back

After handing off the equipment to the next person in line, the first person then goes to the end of the line. This person starts a new relay movement with a new piece of equipment when she reaches the front of the line again.

Special Events

Happy New Year!

The return to school after the holiday break is sometimes difficult for little ones, so before the break, plan a New Year's Celebration.

During the last days of December, send home a note telling parents about your plan. Ask each parent to send in a small treat for a dessert buffet and ask that they send the children to school in pajamas (with rubber-soled slippers or sneakers, for safety).

Explain that you will watch the last 15 minutes of a popular New Year's Eve countdown show (that you have previously taped) and that you will count down to 12:00 (noon). Since many moms and dads await the New Year in their pajamas, the children will be dressed accordingly.

If class money is available, rent a helium tank and fill a balloon for each child. These are at their tables when the children arrive. The children have been away for at least a week, and the decorations help to chase away those "I want to stay home" blues.

Have the children prepare for the countdown by making hats and noisemakers. Introduce them to the word "buffet" and show them how to help themselves to small portions of the food provided.

As the ball drops at the stroke of 12:00 (noon), toss confetti, shake your noisemakers, and cheer in the New Year!

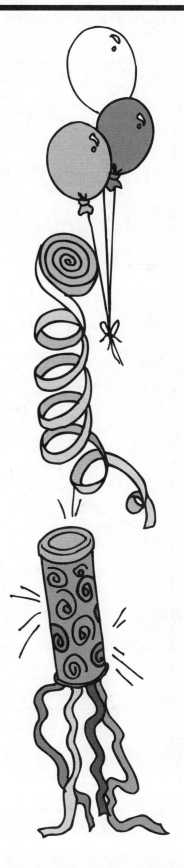

Noisemakers

Noisemakers can be made from recycled half-pint milk containers, small disposable water bottles, potato chip cans, or yogurt cups (with snap-on lids). Wrap the containers in construction paper on which you have written the numerals for the new year. Crepe paper tails can be added for effect. Place a few beans inside for the noise. Just pop on the snap-on lids and you're ready to go.

Confetti

For easy-to-clean up confetti, use coiled paper strips. Demonstrate how to toss the coils. For a quick clean-up, set a timer and allow children one minute to "beat the clock" by putting all of the streamers into a "Happy New Year Basket."

The Groundhog Legend

Name _____

Cut out the sentences. Paste them in the correct order.

He comes out of his burrow.

It is sunny. The groundhog sees his shadow.

He goes back in his burrow for six more weeks of winter.

The groundhog wakes up.

Martin Luther King, Jr.'s, Birthday

The birthday of Martin Luther King, Jr., is observed nationally on the third Monday of January. Celebrate this special event in your classroom using these activities.

Cooperative Learning

Materials needed per pair: glue, crayons, scissors, pencil, piece of 9" x 12" (22.8 cm x 30.4 cm) drawing paper, piece of 12" x 18" (30.4 cm x 45.7 cm) light-colored construction paper

Have students work in pairs for this activity. Instruct students to have one partner draw a simple person figure on a folded piece of drawing paper. Have the other partner cut out the drawing, producing two people figures that are the same. Each partner then colors one figure to look like himself and both figures are glued onto the construction paper. Then have the pairs of students discuss what makes them alike and different. Have them write about it on the construction paper. Hang up the figures for a colorful display titled "Alike and Different."

Art

Martin Luther King, Jr., believed that all people should be treated equally, regardless of the color of their skin. Have each student trace his hand ten times on different colors (except black) and textures of paper. Instruct students to cut out each handprint and glue it in the form of a collage on a large sheet of black construction paper.

Bulletin Board Activity

Martin Luther King, Jr., was a man of peace. Use this activity to encourage peace in the classroom. Ask your class, How can we make our classroom a peaceful place? (Children might respond with these ideas: by sharing, by cooperating, by helping others, by being nice, etc.) Make a simple train figure and attach it to a bulletin board. On the engine, print the title "Peace Train." On each car, leave an opening at the top and print one of the ideas the children mentioned. Print each student's name on a colorful 2" x 8" (5 cm x 20.3 cm) strip of paper. Tell your students that you'll be watching for peace-promoting behavior. As you notice children cooperating, sharing, etc., place their name in the corresponding section of the train. At the end of the day, remove all name cards and begin again the following day.

Special Events

Chinese New Year

In China, the color red signifies happiness and good luck. This color predominates in gifts and decorations for the Chinese New Year celebration. Invite your children to make red streamer wands from paper towel tubes. First, have them cover their tubes using red construction paper and tape; then let them tape four streamers to one end. Use the wands in your own parade.

Valentine Necklace

Materials:

- empty cereal boxes or similar weight cardboard
- construction paper (red, pink, and white)
- scissors
- glue

Directions:

1. Cut a 2" (5 cm) heart pattern from an empty cereal box or cardboard for each student.
2. Each child should trace the heart pattern to make 21 hearts from construction paper. Let them choose the colors they want.
3. Show children how to glue a heart on either side of the heart they want for the center of the necklace. Place the bottom points of the second and third hearts in the middle of the center heart, pointing one heart up to the left and one up to the right.
4. Have children continue gluing the hearts together in this way, making two chains of hearts coming from either side of the center heart.
5. When all 21 hearts have been glued together, each child will have a special necklace to wear for Valentine's Day.

Valentine Decoration Cards

Instead of having students send traditional valentines, be creative and have them make valentine decoration cards instead. Show them how to cover a valentine card with clear adhesive plastic to laminate it, glue a bow to the top of the card, and glue a thin ribbon on it for a hanger. Students will enjoy making and giving these valentines.

© McGraw-Hill Children's Publishing 0-7682-2526-4 *Fast Ideas for Busy Teachers*

Valentine Mailbox Madness

Invite students to take part in a valentine relay race to experience the exhilaration of exercise. First, cover three boxes with valentine paper or heart shapes, then cut four mail slots in each. Have students make four valentine hearts each or provide them each with four envelopes or valentine cards. Divide the class into three teams, set the mailboxes at one end of the room, and place a taped starting line at the opposite end of the room. At the specified signal, the first person from each team will run to that team's mailbox, deposit a valentine in each slot, then return to the team line, tagging the next person to run. The game continues in the same manner until one team successfully deposits all the cards in its mailbox.

Loving Hands Valentines

Copy the following poem on a sheet of white paper for each child. Since there are many possible home situations, leave a blank space in the third line as shown. Have the children fill in the missing word or words as they make their valentines.

Helping Hands show lots of love.
I want to do my part.
By helping _____ every day,
I give love from my heart.

Have each student trace around his hand on a sheet of red paper. Draw a heart in the palm of the hand and cut it out. Have students think about whom they help most at home. Write this person's name in the blank space in the poem. Then have the child glue the hand next to the poem and sign his or her name. They'll enjoy taking the valentine home and giving it to the person whose name is in the poem.

Valentine Door Knob Hanger

Use the pattern on page 126 to make Valentine Doorknob hangers that can be given in place of Valentine cards.

1. Color the doorknob hanger and cut it out.
2. Fold in on the broken lines.
3. Glue together to form a pocket as shown.
4. Fill the pocket with treats such as gum and candy.
5. Hang the valentine on a friend's doorknob.

Valentine Doorknob Hanger

Happy Valentine's Day

You Are Special to Me!

© McGraw-Hill Children's Publishing

126

0-7682-2526-4 *Fast Ideas for Busy Teachers*

The Lion and the Lamb

When March rolls in
With a ferocious growl,
When the temperatures drop
And those cold winds howl,

Then March will exit
In a gentle way
Like a sweet, little lamb
Who has come out to play.

Art

Help students make these simple puppets that can be used in a variety of ways including bulletin board decorations. Staple together two paper plates with a large craft stick in the middle to use as a puppet. On one side of the plate, make the face of a lamb. On the other side, make a lion. Use construction paper, felt, and markers. Use cotton balls for the lamb's wool and yarn for the lion's mane. Recite the poem, having children turn the puppet to the correct side as you say each verse.

Math

Discuss springtime temperatures. Have children show on a thermometer what the temperature might be at the beginning of the month and at the end of the month if the lines of the poem prove to be correct.

Creative Writing

Have students write a story about the March lion. Encourage them to use descriptive words in their stories.

Productive Thinking

The lion and the lamb could be considered opposites. Have children think of two other animals that are opposites. Discuss how they are opposites. (Examples: an elephant and a mouse; a rabbit and a turtle.)

Special Events

Have a Green Day!

Ireland is called the "Emerald Isle" because of its beautiful green countryside. The color green is associated with Ireland, and on Saint Patrick's Day, green is seen everywhere—on clothing, decorations, cakes, and other items.

Have a "Green Day" in your classroom. Here are some suggestions: Let the students display paper shamrocks, green paper chains, and other decorations around the classroom. Have the children do their work on green paper and write with green-colored pencils. Use green chalk to write on the chalkboard and mark your students' papers in green ink.

A "Pot of Gold"

This treasure hunt takes some preparation, but it's well worth the effort. Before school, hide a bowl of treats somewhere at school where the children will not stumble upon it accidentally. (For treats, use items such as gold stickers, candy wrapped in gold foil, or a box of crackers you've wrapped in gold paper.) Tape little paper feet all around the school, making a path from your classroom to the treasure.

Then tell your students you think a leprechaun has visited their room. Explain that leprechauns are creatures believed to have pots of gold. The Irish thought a person who caught a leprechaun had a chance of getting some gold. Point to the trail of footprints, and then let the children follow the path to the treasure. Afterwards, share the treats with the class.

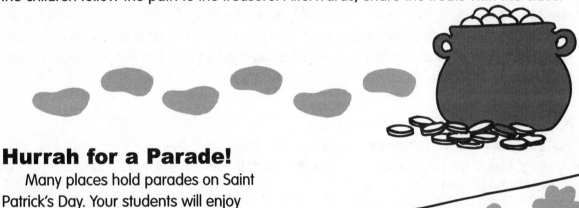

Hurrah for a Parade!

Many places hold parades on Saint Patrick's Day. Your students will enjoy having a parade of their own. Have them make flags by decorating green sheets of paper or gluing green shamrocks onto white construction paper. These can then be taped to cardboard handles. Play some lively Irish music and have students march around the room (or the school) with their flags.

Find the Shamrocks

Name _____

Look at the picture carefully. Can you find the six hidden shamrocks? Color the picture.

Special Events

Easter Relay Races

Give standard relay races a new twist by using an Easter theme:
- Carry plastic eggs on plastic spoons.
- Roll a plastic egg with your nose.
- Leap like a lamb.
- Run with a plastic egg between your knees.

Bunny Hop Circle

Try this version of the bunny hop. Have all the students sit in a circle. Have one student begin by doing one cycle—right foot, right foot, left foot, left foot, forward hop, backward hop, forward hop, hop, hop—of the bunny hop around the outside of a circle. Whoever the first bunny stops behind on the last hop gets to join the back of the bunny hop line. (You may want to start two students at different parts of the circle for a shorter hopping session.) After everyone is in the bunny hop line, remove a bunny from the front of the line at the end of each cycle. Continue until all bunnies are sitting down.

Hop and Count

Your students will have a hopping good time practicing their counting skills. Tape 11 shapes to the floor, each numbered with a different numeral from 0 to 10. Provide each student with a bunny-eared headband. Let the students take turns hopping in sequence as the rest of the students count from 0 to 10.

Feed the Bunny

For a spring activity, add a bunny face to the front of several paper lunch bags. Cut out several pink paper bunny noses and write a number word, a numeral, or an addition or subtraction fact on each nose. Have the students help you in making a number of orange paper carrot cutouts. Attach a pink nose to each bunny bag and place the bags and carrots in your math center. Have pairs of students take turns reading the information on each bunny's nose and depositing the appropriate number of carrots into the bag.

April Showers Mobile

Materials:

- construction paper
- hole punch
- dark crayon
- patterns (see page 132)
- scissors
- cardboard
- glue
- yarn

Directions:

1. Fold a large piece of construction paper in half lengthwise. Punch several holes along the bottom and two holes at the top, as shown.
2. Use a black or dark blue crayon to print "April Showers" on one side of the folded paper. On the other side, print "Bring May Flowers."
3. Using the patterns found on page 132, cut out several raindrops, flowers, and umbrellas. (You'll need to cut the pieces for the flowers and umbrellas from different colors, then glue them together.)
4. Punch a hole in the top of each raindrop, flower, and umbrella.
5. Cut a strip of cardboard and glue it between the folded construction paper to give it stability.
6. Connect the raindrops and umbrellas to the April side of the caption strip with yarn.
7. Connect the flowers to the May side of the caption strip with yarn.
8. Cut some small raindrops from blue paper and glue them on the April side of the strip. Glue some flowers to the May side of the strip.
9. Tie yarn to the holes at the top of the strip and hang up.

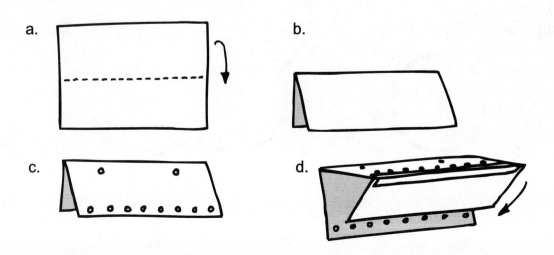

a.

b.

c.

d.

April Showers Mobile Patterns

© McGraw-Hill Children's Publishing

132

0-7682-2526-4 *Fast Ideas for Busy Teachers*

Parading for Our Planet

Share the spirit of Earth Day by having a parade in honor of planet Earth. Make signs that show your support for keeping the Earth clean and unpolluted. Warn your co-workers of this delightful disruption before you parade through the school singing the "Earth Day Anthem."

No Earth Day celebration would be complete without a catchy tune. Use (and reuse) this recycled version of "London Bridge is Falling Down" with your class.

"Earth Day Anthem"

Reduce, reuse, recycle	Care for Earth and keep it clean,
For our Earth,	Keep it clean,
For our Earth.	Keep it clean.
Reduce, reuse, recycle	Care for Earth and keep it clean
For our Earth	Every day.

Palatable Planets

Nothing will be left to recycle when your students make and eat these yummy Earth Day treats. Slice and bake one roll of refrigerated sugar cookie dough. Mix blue food coloring into a can of vanilla frosting until it's a medium shade of blue. Give a cookie to each student. Using craft sticks or plastic knives, have students spread blue frosting on their cookies to represent the oceans. Have them create land areas by placing groupings of mini chocolate chips in the frosting. It's a small (tasty) world.

Special Events

Arbor Day Fun

National Arbor Day is celebrated the last Friday in April. Celebrate in your class by teaching your students the song below. Then make a copy of the tree for each child to complete. To get children started thinking about the usefulness of trees, read aloud the book *The Giving Tree* by Shel Silverstein (HarperCollins, 1986). Mount the trees on a wall with the caption "Tree-ific!"

"Arbor Day Song"

(Sung to the tune of: "I'm a Little Teapot")

I'm a little green tree; water me.
I'll grow as tall as I can be.
I will clean the air and give you shade.
Plant more of me on Arbor Day!

Trees give us_____
and _____

Doggie in the Window

Celebrate National Pet Week in May with this fun art activity. You'll need a 9" x 12" (22.8 cm x 30.4 cm) sheet of white paper for each student, magazine pictures of dogs, markers, glue, and scissors.

1. Fold the paper in half to measure 9" x 6" (22.8 cm x 15.2 cm).
2. Cut a large rectangular window in the front flap of the folded paper.
3. Write "Pet Shop" above the window.
4. Open the paper and glue a dog picture to the center of the back flap.
5. Use markers to draw toys, bones, a food bowl, etc., around the dog.
6. Refold the paper and you'll see the dog in the pet shop window.
7. Open the paper, and you've brought the doggie home.

Pet Shirts

Your students will love making shirts for their favorite stuffed pets. Purchase inexpensive baby undershirts from a thrift store. Have the children use fabric markers or fabric paint to print their pets' names on the shirts and decorate them.

Pets Throughout the Year

Take advantage of the pet resources around you. Throughout the year, have your students introduce their pets in person to the class. Even children who are afraid of some animals enjoy experiencing them from a distance. Set aside just ten minutes once a month for a pet visit. Talk with the parent and the students ahead of time about safety. Have the pet owner tell briefly about the pet and how to care for it.

Our Favorite Pets

Do you have pets in your classroom or in other classrooms that the students know and love? During Be Kind to Animals Week in May, let these pets be the stars of sentences, stories, poems, and math problems that you or your students write. Who wouldn't be eager to solve a math story problem about dear little Spot the class rat, or to write a poem about Peaches the cockatiel?

Special Events

Keepsake Print

Celebrate Mother's Day by making a special footprint keepsake for Mom.

Materials:

- eight-inch (20.3 cm) pie tin
- large doily
- plaster of Paris
- 9" x 12" (22.8 cm x 30.4 cm) sheet of construction paper
- crayons or markers
- paper towels for cleanup

Directions:

1. Place the doily inside the pie tin.
2. Mix the plaster by following the directions on the package.
3. Pour the plaster on top of the doily.
4. Have a child place his/her bare foot in the plaster and gently press down.
5. Clean the child's foot with paper towels.
6. Have children fold the construction paper to make a card for their mothers. Have them write "Thank you for guiding my footsteps" in the card. Decorate the card and sign it.

Flower Picture Frame

Have children trace the flower pattern on page 137 on a folded sheet of construction paper. Have them cut out the flower on the fold. Then have them trace and cut leaves from green paper. Glue leaves at the sides of the flowers. Each student should then cut a 2" (5 cm) circle from construction paper and glue his school photo on it. The photo circle may then be glued to the center of the flower and this poem printed inside the flower.

I am like a flower
That's raised with love by you.
You help me grow up big and strong.
Mom, thanks for all you do.

Flower and Leaf Patterns

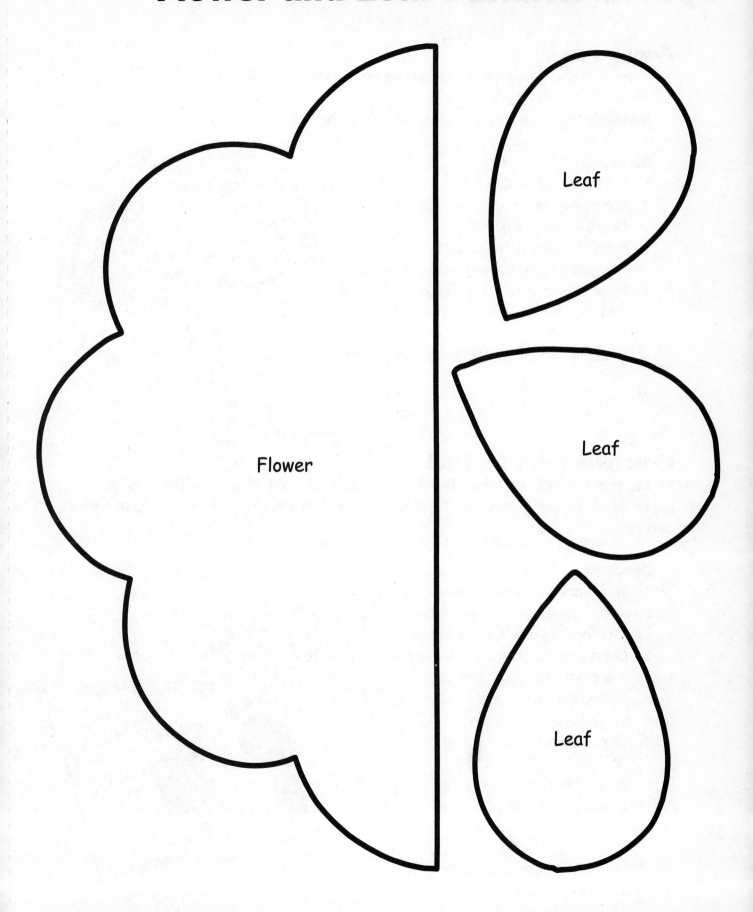

Flower

Leaf

Leaf

Leaf

137 0-7682-2526-4 *Fast Ideas for Busy Teachers*

Special Events

Fancy Fan

Here's a Mother's Day gift that is easy for young children to make.

Materials: thin paper plate, scissors, wide craft stick, glue, markers, crayons, or paint

Directions:
1. Cut the paper plate in half.
2. Flatten the halves as much as possible. Glue the halves together.
3. Before the glue dries, insert a craft stick between the two halves to make a handle.
4. Write a message such as the one shown on your fan (or glue on a preprinted message).

Decorate the fan with markers, crayons, or paint.

Precious Print for Dad

Materials: shallow container, 11" x 17" (27.9 cm x 43.1 cm) sheet of white construction paper, black tempera paint, black felt-tip marker, laminating plastic, paper towels for cleanup.

Directions:
1. Pour black paint into a shallow container.
2. Step into the paint with one foot and press your footprint onto the white paper.
3. Clean your foot with a wet paper towel. Make a print of your other foot, placing the second footprint beside the first one.
4. Clean the second foot. Allow the paint to dry.
5. Write on the paper above the footprints, "Dear Daddy, I want to follow in your footsteps by _____. Love, _____."
6. Laminate the project or cover it with clear adhesive paper.

Scratchy Notepad

Materials: notepad, sandpaper, crayons, glue, scissors, pencil, stamp pad

Preparation: Cut a rectangle of sandpaper for each child. The rectangle should be a half-inch (1.2 cm) longer than two times the length plus the depth of the notepad. It should be a half-inch (1.2 cm) wider than the notepad.

Directions:

1. Use crayons to decorate the sandpaper. Press hard.
2. Put glue on the back of the notepad. Position it on the back of the sandpaper 1/4 inch (.63 cm) from the bottom edge.
3. Fold the sandpaper over the top of the notepad. Crease at the two folds to make it stay down.
4. Write a note to Dad on the first page of the notepad. Decorate the note with your thumbprint.

Flashy Tie

This oversized tie will have Dad grinning from ear to ear on Father's Day. For an extra-special surprise, have each child make two—one for Dad and a matching one for herself.

Materials: 24-inch-long (60.9 cm) necktie shape (with a knot) cut from white butcher paper, 2" x 26" (5 cm x 66 cm) white butcher-paper band, tempera paints, paintbrushes, stapler, glue

Directions: After discussing common tie designs such as stripes, dots, flowers, and paisleys, have the students paint the tie shape and band with their favorite designs. When the paint is dry, size the band to fit over an adult's head and staple the ends together. Center the knot of the tie over the staple and glue the tie to the band.

Special Events

Year-in-Review Mural

This display will remind your students of the great year they've had and all they've learned in your class. Hang butcher paper around your room. (Divide the paper into as many sections as there are months in the school year and label them. Brainstorm with the students a list of fun things that happened in each month and write them under the appropriate month's heading. (Use your lesson plans to prompt memories.) Leave enough room for students to decorate.

To decorate the mural, each student can illustrate one activity, glue on an art project from a specific month, add a photograph, or do whatever she can to illustrate the learning that took place during a specific month. Encourage memories and creativity.

Hats-off-to-School Day

Designate a day when each person wears his favorite, biggest, funniest, silliest, or most unusual hat. Discuss the different hats. Categorize them by various attributes (size, color, use, etc.), then have the students hold up their hats and shout, "Hats off to school!"

Parent Tea

Put on a small program for parents at the year's end. Students can sing songs and recite poems they've learned during the year. Keep refreshments simple enough for the students to serve their own guests.

Class Fun Day

Schedule a day of fun. Set up six stations (example: Bean Bag Toss; Peanut-in-the-Spoon Race; Wheelbarrow Race; Sweep-a-Potato-With-a-Broom Race; Water Balloon Toss; Try On and Rehang Clothes on a Clothesline Race). Place students in six groups. Ask parents to help with the events. Be sure to have snacks and drinks afterwards.

Camping in the Classroom

This is a wonderful "Theme Day" activity for the end of the year—the kids will love it.

Transform your classroom into a campsite complete with tents, sleeping bags, and an artificial campfire. The campfire can be made with real logs and paper flames. You can also create a river from paper and bring in artificial Christmas trees for a woodsy feel.

Encourage students to bring in any stuffed animals that they might find in the woods such as bears, raccoons, deer, etc. Set them around the campground. Turn this into a creative writing experience by asking students to write about an experience they might have with one of these animals.

Allow students to dress as they would in the woods and bring in camping gear such as their sleeping bags, flashlights, and fishing rods (without the hooks). To fish, students can cut out paper fish with math problems on them. Each fish has a paper clip attached to it and the fishing lines should have magnets instead of hooks. Students take turns "fishing" and completing the math problems on the fish they catch.

For a special treat, make s'mores in a microwave oven. Copy the words to old songs such as "Old Dan Tucker" and "Camptown Races," put them in song booklets, and sing them around the campfire.

Turn out the lights and pull down the shades. Then have children go into the tents to read books by the light of flashlights. This will give them a chance to rest in their sleeping bags. Play a CD of wilderness sounds during this time.

You'll find that the day goes by much too quickly. Students will get their required classwork completed even though they did it while lying on the floor. What a wonderful experience for everyone.

Special Events

Patriotic Badges

Your class will enjoy making special badges to wear in honor of America's birthday. Give each student a 4" (10.1 cm) circle cut from heavy white paper. Then have students use red and blue markers to decorate the badge with a patriotic design. If you like, give students gummed stars (red, blue, silver) to add to their designs. To finish off the badge, have each student tape a 6" (15.2 cm) loop of ribbon to the back, and attach a safety pin to the loop.

Stars and Stripes Tag

This tag game is fun to play any time during the year! Divide your class into two teams—the Stars and the Stripes. Have the teams stand in two lines, about 30 feet (9.1 cm) apart from each other.

For Round One, have the Stars stand with their backs to the Stripes. At your signal, the Stripes tiptoe up to within two feet of the stars. When you call Run, the Stars turn around and chase the Stripes. Any Stripe who is caught must freeze and stand upright (like a stripe); Stripes who reach their original line are "home free."

For Round Two, have the teams switch roles. Any Star who is caught must freeze and stand with arms and legs outstretched (like a star).

Fruity Delights

Put a scoop of vanilla ice cream or plain yogurt in individual serving dishes. Top with blueberries and sliced strawberries.

Gelatin Cubes

Make red and blue gelatin according to the directions on the package. Pour each mixture into a shallow baking dish and cool until firm. Cut the gelatin into 1" (2.54 cm) cubes. Place each dish briefly in a sink filled with warm water to loosen the gelatin, and then place the cubes in a bowl. Serve in individual dishes. If you like, top with whipped cream.

Fantastic Fireworks

Discuss with students that fireworks are an exciting part of Fourth of July celebrations. Talk about what fireworks look like and the kinds of noises they make as they shoot into the sky. If possible, show pictures of fireworks to the class.

Next, give each student a sheet of black paper and colored chalk. Show them how they can use curved lines and dots to make starbursts on the paper. Then have the class fill their paper with colorful fireworks. Afterwards, take the papers outdoors or to a well-ventilated area and lightly spray them with hair spray to prevent the chalk from rubbing off. Let students take their pictures home to display on Independence Day.

Stories for Independence Day

The following picture books center on Independence Day celebrations:

* *Fourth of July Bear* by Kathryn Lasky (Morrow, 1991). Two children dress up as bears for an exciting Fourth of July parade.
* *Jake Johnson: The Story of a Mule* by Tres Seymour (DK Publishing, 1999). A mule refuses to haul fireworks to the fairgrounds on Independence Day.
* *Hurray for the Fourth of July* by Wendy Watson (Clarion, 1992). A small-town family celebrates the Fourth of July.

Patriotic Visors

Make colorful visors to wear on the Fourth of July. First, reproduce the patterns on page 144 for each student. Have students cut out the visor and stars. Next, have them trace and cut out as many stars as they wish on red or blue paper. Then, have them glue the stars onto the visor. Finally, punch out holes where indicated, and have students tie a 15" (38.1 cm) piece of yarn to each hole.

Patriotic Visor

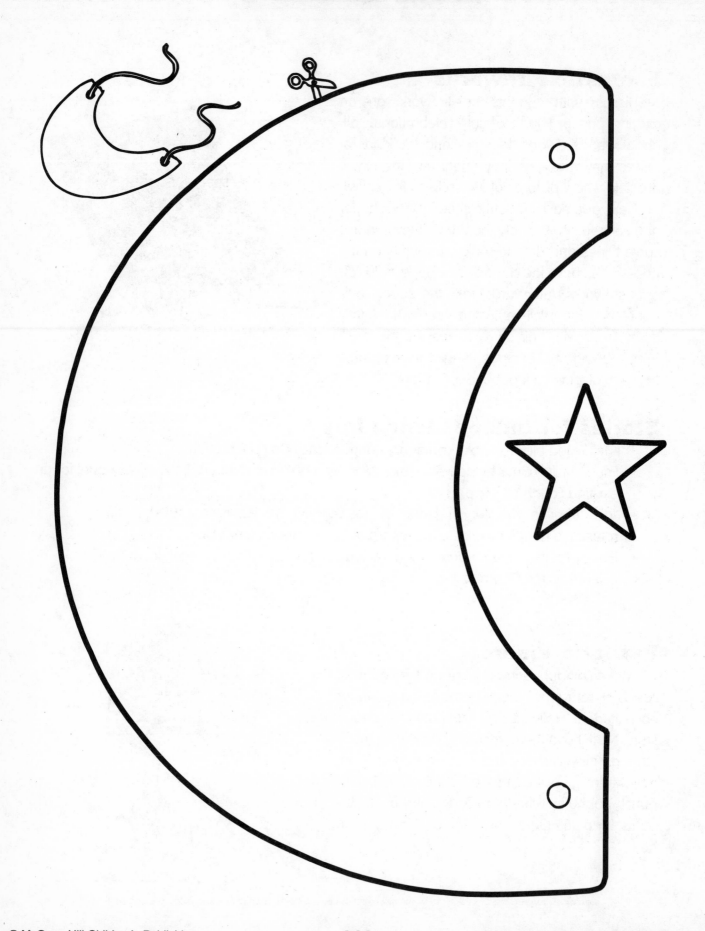

© McGraw-Hill Children's Publishing

144

0-7682-2526-4 *Fast Ideas for Busy Teachers*

First Day of School Penny

Begin class by reading one of the many stories about the first day of school. After reading the book, discuss as a group how children feel about meeting new friends. At this time pass out a "treasure"—a current year's penny. Tell the children, "This is a reminder of your first day of school in the first grade—a one cent coin dated (current year)." End the lesson by telling the children that the penny is, in fact, a magic friend maker and if they keep it safe, they will be sure to make new friends. Have them put the pennies in a special place for the year. Remarkably, many of them will still have the penny and remember the lesson at the end of the school year.

Bag of Goodies to Take Home

As parents leave your back-to-school meeting, give each of them a bag of "goodies" to take home to their child. Enclose in each bag a note to the child about your excitement and wishes for the year ahead.

First Day Journals

On the first day of school, use an instant camera to take individual photos of students. Ask each child to make a journal entry about the first day in your class. Place the photo on the page so the child and her parents will have a special memory of this special day.

My First Day In School

Special Events

"The Secret"

I'm a little green leaf hanging
From a backyard tree.
Shhh! Don't tell, I have a secret.
Soon I'll let you see.

Daylight hours are growing shorter,
The autumn sun's not strong.
My green color is starting to fade.
Watch now, it won't be long.

The chlorophyll that made me green
Soon will disappear.
That's when I'll reveal my secret
For all the world to share.

Surprise! I am a yellow leaf
Still on a backyard tree.
Now you see my hidden color.
It's lovely, lovely me!

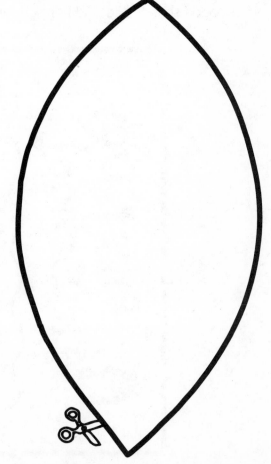

Art

Have children make mosaic autumn leaves from small pieces of cut construction paper. You may want to have them include some pieces of green paper on their leaves. Hang all the leaves on a class tree.

Science

Challenge each child to find and bring to class a leaf that has both green and another color on it. Press the leaves with waxed paper so they can become part of a science center.

Math

Use pictures of colored leaves repetitively to create a sequence pattern. Form patterns using both leaf colors and shapes. Challenge children to figure out the sequence.

Literature

Read *Red Leaf, Yellow Leaf* by Lois Ehlert (Harcourt, 1991).

Pumpkin Puzzle

When your class carves a face in a pumpkin for Halloween, try to use as many geometric shapes as possible—circle nose, triangle eyes, and rectangle mouth. Save the pieces you cut out and have the children fit them back into the pumpkin in the correct spaces, like puzzle pieces.

"Bat-ter" Have a Safe Halloween!

To encourage your students to have a safe Halloween, put this bulletin board up in your room or hall. Use the bat pattern below to make bats from black paper. Discuss Halloween safety rules in class and write the rules on white paper. Put one rule on each of the bats. Cover them with clear adhesive plastic so you can use them for more than one year. Glue craft eyes to the bats and fold the bats outs lightly when you attach them to the board so they are three dimensional.

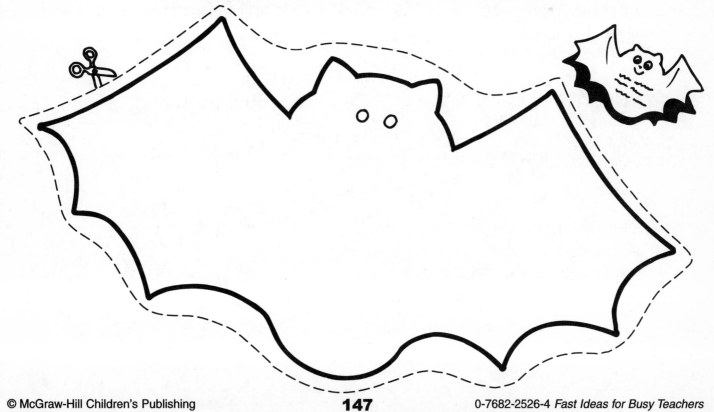

Halloween Addition

Name _____

Read, count and color.

1. Count the 🎃 s
in the 🎃 patch.

2. Count the ▱ es
on the 🧑‍🌾 .

3. How many 🦉 s
are sitting the 🪵 ?

4. How many 🦇 s
are flying away?

5. How many 🕷 s
do you see?

6. Count the 🐱 s
sitting next to the 🐭 .

© McGraw-Hill Children's Publishing
0-7682-2526-4 *Fast Ideas for Busy Teachers*

Fire Safety Mobile

Use this mobile to reinforce fire safety rules during Fire Safety Month in October.
Trace and color. Cut out, punch holes, and tie together.

My Fire Prevention
Safety Pledge

I will never
play with
matches.

I will not
open a
hot door.

I will
practice
fire drills.

I will practice
stop, drop,
and roll.

I promise to do these safe things.

_____

Student's Name

© McGraw-Hill Children's Publishing **149** 0-7682-2526-4 *Fast Ideas for Busy Teachers*

Special Events

"Read and Feed"

Here's a creative way to get your students interested in reading. This works especially well as a display for Book Week in November. Have them make this fun tool for keeping track of the books they read. Copy the pattern below for each child to color and cut out. Each child should write his name on the calf's ear tag. Then have them fold up the bottom part of the pattern and glue it where shown to make a pocket. Have students attach their calves to the bulletin board described on page 151. As students read books, have them print the book titles on bales of hay and put the hay in the pocket to "feed" their calves.

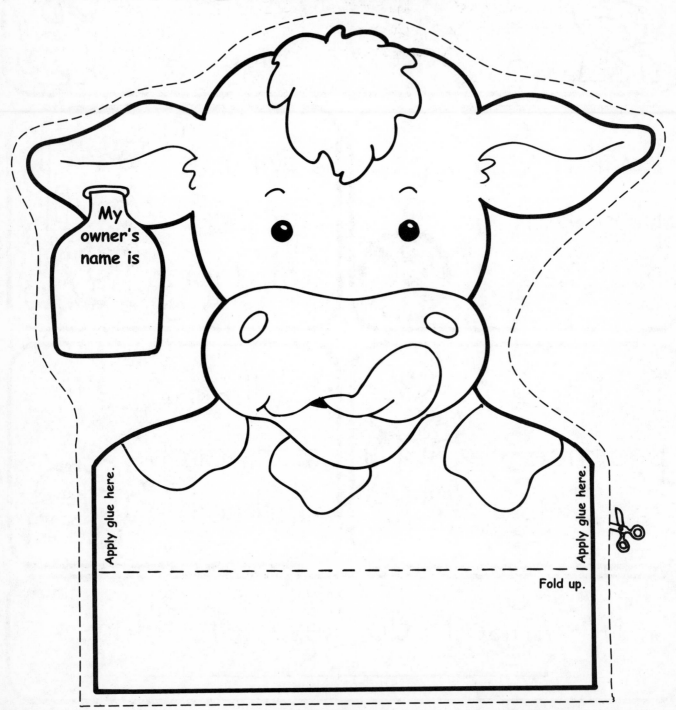

Make multiple copies of the hay bales on yellow or light green paper and cut them out. Draw two large barns on red paper and cut them out. Cut a large window out of one barn (large enough for the hay bales to fit inside easily). Then staple the two barns together. Mount the barn at the center of a bulletin board. Put a good supply of hay bales inside the barn for students to use to record books they read.

Cut out the feed sack and attach it to the bulletin board to remind students of what they should do and why. Make a border of farm-related pictures or items around the bulletin board.

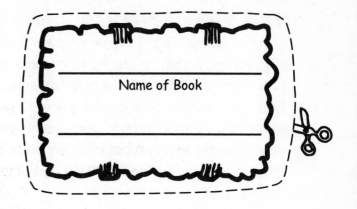

Name of Book

Read and Feed

Read and Feed
1. Read a good book.
2. Write the name of the book on a bale of hay from the barn.
3. Place the bale in the feed trough under your calf's head.

Important!
• Do not let your calf starve; feed it often.

© McGraw-Hill Children's Publishing

0-7682-2526-4 *Fast Ideas for Busy Teachers*

Special Events

The First Thanksgiving

Discuss the origin of our traditional Thanksgiving, a three-day feast shared by the Pilgrims and Native Americans in celebration of a successful harvest. Talk about and list various kinds of food that were probably served then and those that most probably were not. Examples of food items probably shared at the time might include: pumpkin, corn, beans, wild turkey, venison, dried berries, cornbread, and fish. Items that were probably not available at that time might include: ice cream, beef, ham, cake, soda, oranges, bananas, and other more modern foods. Provide the children with magazines, scissors, and glue. Have them cut out food pictures into "Then" and "Now" groups, and glue each group to an individual poster board chart labeled accordingly. Talk about which of the foods would be the healthiest.

Pilgrim Day

For Pilgrim Day, plan several activities related to the first Thanksgiving. Ask parents to help with outfits either at home or at school. Keep on hand various outfits just in case a child doesn't have one. Keep it simple, such as paper Native American headbands and sack vests, white-paper Pilgrim collars, and white dishtowel Pilgrim aprons. Then let your students use their imaginations as they build a model of a Plymouth village. Use boxes, toy building logs, and plastic trees, fences, and animals. Make stand-up figures of Pilgrims and Native Americans by reproducing images from a book and gluing them to wooden blocks. For a writing lesson, post a large paper tree without leaves on the wall. Encourage the children to think of something they are thankful for. Help each child write it on a precut leaf shape and attach the leaf to the tree. Then it's time to eat. Have a simple feast prepared including such things as pieces of turkey, cranberry bread, corn bread, and pumpkin pie. After eating, lead a Pilgrim Day parade through the rest of your school so that others can enjoy your celebration.

Turkey Basket

1. Color the turkey pattern and cut it out.
2. Fold on the broken lines.
3. Glue the tabs to the front and back of the turkey basket as shown.
4. Glue the "Be Thankful!" tail to the rest of the turkey's tail on the inside, as shown.
5. Fill your turkey basket with Thanksgiving treats such as candy or cookies.

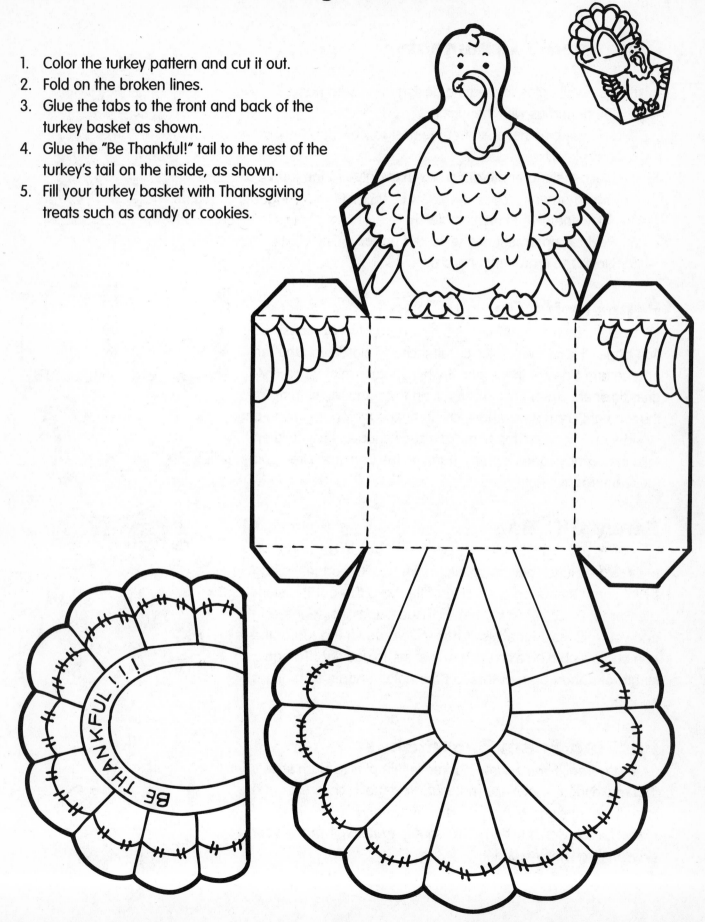

BE THANKFUL!!!

© McGraw-Hill Children's Publishing

0-7682-2526-4 *Fast Ideas for Busy Teachers*

Special Events

Pine Needle Ornaments

1. Use white glue to create a design on waxed paper. (Be generous with the glue.)
2. Sprinkle pine needles over the design, covering the glue completely.
3. Place a string or metal hanger in the glue at the top of the ornament.
4. Allow the glue to dry completely.
5. Peel the ornament off the waxed paper.
6. Hang the ornament on the tree.

Peppermint Candy Cane

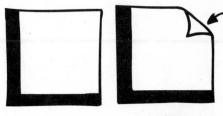

Give each child an 8" (20. 3 cm) square of white construction paper. Have them color a half-inch red border on the left and bottom sides of the paper. Sprinkle peppermint oil on children's papers. Then have them roll up their papers, starting at the top right corner. Next have children glue their papers into a cylinder and bend the top to make a cane shape. Have children take their candy canes home to hang on the Christmas tree and make the room smell nice.

Fancy Gift Bag

Here's a simple, decorative gift bag. Choose an appropriately colored lunch bag or a plain brown bag. Decorate the bag by tracing a stencil on each side of the bag. Cut out the stenciled area. Place a solid sheet of tissue paper inside the bag and your gift inside the tissue paper. Fold down the top of the bag and punch a hole on each side of the folded flap. Thread a length of ribbon or yarn through the holes and tie to make a handle.

Packing Foam Snowflakes

Many fragile items come packed in thin plastic foam sheets that make ideal snowflake material. Have each child cut out a snowflake design, glue on glitter, and attach a length of monofilament for hanging. This snowy touch will make your classroom a winter wonder.

© McGraw-Hill Children's Publishing 0-7682-2526-4 *Fast Ideas for Busy Teachers*

Candy Canes

Trace or draw a candy cane on white poster board or heavy paper. Cut out the shape and punch a hole at the top. Use markers to draw on stripes. Set the candy cane on a piece of waxed paper. Spread glue around the edges of the candy cane; then sprinkle glitter on the glue. After the glue dries, shake off the excess glitter. Tie ribbon around the candy cane and attach a jingle bell. To hang your candy cane, tie a string through the hole on the top.

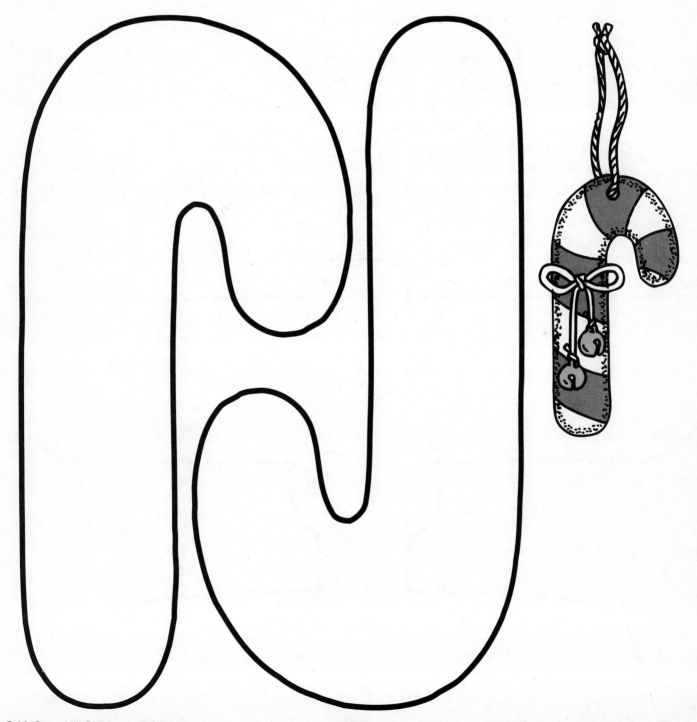

Special Events ——————————

Shiny Menorah

Make a foil-covered menorah that stands.

Materials: pattern found below, sheet of cardboard, white and orange construction paper, gold foil wrapping paper, glue, scissors

Directions:

1. Cut out the menorah pattern. Trace the pattern on cardboard and cut it out.
2. Cut nine candles out of white construction paper and nine oval flames out of orange construction paper.
3. Glue one flame to the top of each candle. Glue the candles on the cardboard menorah.
4. Cover the cardboard menorah with foil. Glue the foil in place. Cut two 3/4-inch (1.9 cm) slits at the bottom of the menorah.
5. Wrap a piece of foil around a 1/2-inch x 6-inch (1.2 cm x 15.2 cm) strip of cardboard. Slide each end of the strip into one of the slits in the menorah to make the menorah stand up.

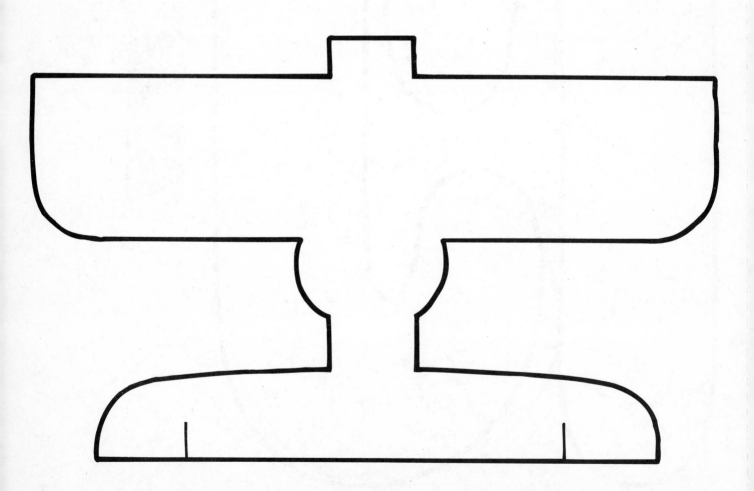

Johnny Appleseed Party

Have a class party to honor John Chapman (Johnny Appleseed) on his birth date of September 26. If possible, visit an orchard or have someone from your local agriculture department visit with students. During this time, students can touch apples, weigh apples, draw pictures of apples, smell and taste different apples, and sort and count seeds.

On the big day, have students wear shirts with apples pictured on them or the colors of apples (green, red, or yellow). Make apple birthday crowns from construction paper. Tell the story of Johnny Appleseed and look at maps to plot his trek across the United States. Students can also create apple birthday cards and make applesauce in the classroom. Have parents wash, core, and slice apples. Put the apples in a pot of water to cook. Students can take turns stirring the mixture until the slices are mush. Divide the mixture and add cinnamon to half of it. When it's cool, students can eat the applesauce and compare the two flavors.

Sing songs such as "Happy Birthday" and "There Was a Fruit that Grew on a Tree" to the tune of "Bingo." Tape-record the children singing, then replay it for the class. This activity is a great deal of fun and will generate lots of laughs.

Let students create their own party favors by cutting out apple patterns, printing **A** words on them and making necklaces or apple ornaments.

Special Events

Lucky Pair Party

According to Chinese tradition, even numbers bring good luck and two of anything makes for double the luck and happiness. Talk with your students about familiar things that come in pairs, such as body parts, clothing, salt and pepper shakers, and so on. Set aside a special Pair Day at school. On this day, use only two colors for drawing and painting, have the children bring in a pair of something for show and tell, and serve crackers and fruit pieces in pairs for a snack.

"Beary" Special Day

Select one day out of the school year to have a Teddy Bear Tea Party. Students bring their stuffed bears (provide extras for those who don't have bears). Celebrate by snacking on bear-shaped cookies, candies, and other treats. Invite parents and grandparents in to read books about bears to the class. During the last 30 minutes of the day, let each child read a book to his bear.

Nutrition Party

Each child brings in one healthy snack. Then take all of the fruits and cut them up into a fruit salad. The children will enjoy cutting the soft fruits such as bananas and canned pineapple with plastic knives.

Place all the children's chairs in a circle, facing out. On each chair, put a picture of a food. Children dance around the chairs while music plays. When the music stops, they sit in the chairs and put the food pictures on their laps. One food in the group is "junk food" (usually a picture of candy or cake). The child with the junk food becomes the D.J. and gets to turn the next song on and off until someone else gets the "junk food."

Pajama Party!

Students wear their pajamas, including slippers, to school. Have them bring their blankets or whatever they sleep with, including night-lights. Plug in the night-lights into available sockets (rotate if you have to), serve hot chocolate and cookies as a "bedtime snack," turn out the lights (except the night-lights), and tell the children "bedtime stories." The children pretend to sleep and when they "wake up," it will be time for school again. Hold a pajama fashion show when the children wake up.

Water Day

When the school year is almost finished and the days are very hot, try this celebration made up of various stations that the students can rotate through.

Bubble Making

Have children use string, straws, and plastic holders that six packs of soda cans come in to make different-sized bubbles.

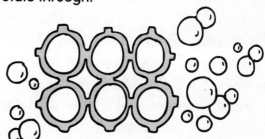

Wading Pool

Let children play in a wading pool filled with water and donated water toys.

Sun Visors

At this station, the children make sun visors out of construction paper and tied with yarn or elastic.

Sunglasses

Here the children can make sunglasses out of construction paper, cut out the eye sections and cover them with colored plastic wrap.

Water Races

The children can have races erasing pictures drawn with chalk on the sidewalk by using spray bottles to shoot water at the pictures.

159

Special Events

Alarming Fun

Though most of your students may not know how to tell time, plan a special day to celebrate clocks and alarms. Bring several different kinds of clocks to class. Set the alarms to go off at different times. Students will enjoy the noise. Talk about why we need clocks with alarms. Ask how many children's families use alarm clocks to wake them in the morning. Ask children to suggest other kinds of alarms (roosters, whistles, bells, etc.). Point out that barking dogs are alarms that tell us when someone is at the door or in the yard. What features does an alarm need? It needs to be loud and persistent. If possible, demonstrate a watch alarm. Point out that it isn't very loud, but it is persistent, continuing until the wearer turns it off. Let children make up their own alarms and demonstrate them.

Celebrating Differences

Have children notice how they are different from one another in a variety of ways—hair color, eye color, likes and dislikes, etc. Point out that if everyone were exactly the same, life would be boring and a lot less fun. Then sing the following song together. (Tune: "Did You Ever See a Lassie?")

I'm so glad that we're all different,
We're different, so different.
I'm so glad that we're all different.
We're not all the same.
We're different in size and in color and clothing.
I'm so glad that we're all different.
We're not all the same.

Cool School Party

Have a party to celebrate school. Invite parents, grandparents, and friends, as well as your school principal. Decorate the room with cutouts of a school bus, a picture of the school, and photos of your children doing schoolwork and enjoying special activities. Ask each child to tell why she thinks school is cool. They might mention a favorite activity, describe a special field trip, or talk about a new friend. Have them say the following rap together for their guests.

School is cool! (clap, clap, clap)
It's fun every day! (stomp, stomp, stomp)
We use our brains (hold hands in air and shake head left and right)
And then we play! (jump up and down)
School (clap, clap, clap)
Is (stomp, stomp, stomp)
Cool! (jump up and shout "Yeah!")